CW01468599

My Wide World of

SPORTS

By Tom Schuman

To my wife, Karen, who has put up with me –
both inside and outside the sports world – for so many years.

For Megan, Josh, Nate and little Chloe.

To my brother Gary and sister Diane, and
two wonderful parents who were always there for all of us.

Contents

MY WIDE WORLD OF SPORTS

O K, it wasn't the first memory from my childhood, or even the second or third. But you have to admit it had a catchy beat – and a classic opening. And I had no idea at the time of the importance of what took place on this Saturday afternoon tradition.

"It" was the *Wide World of Sports*. One week, it was cliff diving from Acapulco; the next might be daredevil Evil Knievel attempting his latest motorcycle jump (Snake Canyon may have been my favorite). The show also featured some of the first U.S. television coverage of Wimbledon, the Indianapolis 500, the Little League World Series and much more.

Longtime host Jim McKay welcomed viewers with the following: "Spanning the globe to bring you the constant variety of sports ... the thrill of victory ... and the agony of defeat ... the human drama of athletic competition. This is ABC's Wide World of Sports."

Watching those far-flung events and competitions was a weekly adventure. Was it responsible for what became a personal lifelong love affair with sports? Probably not. But it's a perfect metaphor of what my life would become – playing (a little), working in, going to, watching and experiencing a "wide world of sports" in so many ways.

I love sports. I love my wife, children and family a whole lot more (although they might dispute that at times). My first job as a teen was as a baseball and softball umpire. My first "real" job was as a sportswriter. The writing career evolved into news and business, but sports never really exited the picture. The American love affair with

1

bats, balls, pucks, clubs and more bridged the gap in many successful interviews.

The first date for Karen, my wife of now 36-plus years, and I was a Cincinnati Reds Opening Day game. It is only a slight exaggeration that we say "our song" is the National Anthem.

It is also abundantly clear that this was a team effort. Karen has provided numerous examples over the years of her sports passion and knowledge – often to the amazement of others. One of the best anecdotes of how lucky I am, and have been for many years, came during our final baseball road trip of 2022.

Exiting Truist Park in Atlanta following a night game, a statue lurked in the distance. As we walked closer, Karen offered that the pitching form in the darkness could be Phil Niekro. Impressive enough right there. But she then saw the knuckleball grip featured in the pitcher's windup and confirmed (not asked) that indeed the statue had to be the Hall of Fame pitcher known as "Knucksie," who won 318 games in 24 years in the majors (20 with the Milwaukee/Atlanta Braves).

We have enjoyed the true pleasure of attending a wide variety of events – amazingly diverse in both their content and location. The stories and the memories are numerous.

I have spent my life telling others' stories as a journalist. It's been a wonderful ride. Along the way, I've accumulated a few tales of my own that I think you might enjoy.

INTRODUCTION

In 1989 in an Iowa cornfield, Kevin Costner heard the words: "If you build it, he will come."

It was 33 years later, in June 2022, when Karen and I came to that Field of Dreams site in Dyersville (if you haven't been there, it's not easy to get to but well worth it).

We were able to make this special visit on a hot summer day. The stay lasted less than two hours. But we walked on the field where the ghosts of Shoeless Joe Jackson and the Chicago Black Sox came back to life in the movie. In contrast to the past, we could see the future as in the construction of the temporary stadium where the Cincinnati Reds and Chicago Cubs would play the second Field of Dreams major league game in August.

What was billed as a tour of the house featured in the movie was so much more – as in a 40-minute history lesson on the farm, the movie and what all this means to Iowans. The "professor" was Craig who, quite ironically, began his career as a sportswriter. He later became a news reporter at the local newspaper and now was a full-time prophet of this historical location.

We learned so much in such a short time

In the Iowa cornfields at the Field of Dreams.

frame. A few examples:

- The plan of movie producers to bring in artificial corn was dismissed by local leaders who instead utilized fire trucks and additional methods to ensure the corn would be at its proper height for filming.
- Tom Hanks turned down the Costner role and the original title, *Shoeless Joe*, fared so poorly in focus group tests that that name was changed to the iconic *Field of Dreams*.
- Actor Dwier Brown, who played John Kinsella (the father of Costner's character) in the closing scene had to overcome his own personal tragedy as his father had passed away a short time before filming. The emotion from Brown in his role was real.

There were additional stories behind some of the items in the house. The souvenir shop was a little disappointing, but this was about the hallowed ground that means so much more than just baseball. (But we both opted for some overpriced T-shirts anyway).

This was the proverbial icing on the cake to an unbelievable 2022. It was Karen and I's first full year of both retirement and living in our new home in Arizona (both occurred in the middle of a hectic period in 2021).

But what really made 2022 so special for the purpose of this book is our "return" to numerous sports events and activities after two years dominated by COVID. The tragedy that impacted so many largely kept us – and countless others – at home.

So, put the two together – much more time to travel in retirement and a yearning for both old and new sports experiences – and we have a year to remember.

There's a trifecta that we're claiming we may have been the only two people to experience. It took us from Las Vegas to Omaha to Eugene, Oregon. True sports fans will know the annual event in one of those cities and likely can surmise what we witnessed in the "track capital of the world." Full details to come in Chapter 17.

There was an intricately planned conclusion to our quest to visit all 30 major league baseball stadiums. That involved three separate journeys – one to Kansas City; a second to Seattle and Oakland; and a final trio in Atlanta, Miami and Tampa-St. Pete. We'll share some of the experiences from those cities and the other stadiums we visited across the country.

There was an unexpected, but truly emotional run to the Super Bowl by my beloved Cincinnati Bengals. When your favorite team hasn't won even a playoff game in more than 30 years, three postseason victories in as many weeks are certainly worthy of celebration. There will be much more about the highs (a few anyway) and the way too many lows of this passion.

I was able to return to a NCAA Final Four basketball tradition with a second trip to New Orleans. A dozen years of reuniting with my two best friends (plus adding a few more pals from time to time) has taken us from Indianapolis, Houston and Dallas to Phoenix, San Antonio and Minneapolis. Maybe the top in-person sports ending for me falls into this category.

But that, of course, is not where it all began.

CHAPTER 1

Read All About It

In addition to watching *Wide World of Sports*, life in the small town (think 600 people) of St. Leon, Indiana (German Catholic community 30 miles from downtown Cincinnati) consisted of playing whatever sport was in season. A goal in the driveway, a large yard and plenty of friends nearby allowed for a rotating mix of basketball, baseball and football.

As 6-year-olds we traveled to nearby towns for Pee Wee baseball. One destination – Stateline – had its field named after former major league outfielder Jim Lytle. As a slightly – OK, more than slightly – wild left-hander, I recall pitching a one-hitter. A few walks and hit batters were part of the mix as we only lost 11-10.

In middle school, I was one of the leading scorers on our basketball team. By the end of my freshman year, my combination of being too small and too slow was exposed. I did participate in four years of high school tennis, winning a conference title in doubles my junior year.

But the biggest development in those days came off the field or court. The twice-weekly county newspaper was looking for a correspondent to cover high school sports. I was attending most of the games anyway, so why not write some stories and earn a little money while doing it? Little did I know that would be the beginning of a long career.

The East Central High School teams I covered were mediocre at best. Which, looking back on it, would probably be an apt description for the articles I submitted. I recall they were often lengthy and filled with the proper facts and quotes, but largely lacking in overall quality.

For a couple of years, our basketball coach was the son of Indiana's bellowed governor, Otis "Doc" Bowen. As a reminder that it's who you know, Rick Bowen was an assistant coach two years later in the Big Ten (following friend Steve Yoder to Wisconsin from Ball State University).

I also wrote for the high school newspaper during that time, which was supervised by English teacher Roger Bear. More than 40 years later, I was interviewing Indiana's superintendent of public instruction for an Indiana Chamber podcast. The conversation turned to the important role of teachers, and I mentioned Roger Bear as an early influence for me.

A few hours after the podcast aired, I had a voicemail from Bear, who had left my high school before our senior year for a career that featured ministry work in college athletics. A friend of his heard the interview and let him know his name was mentioned. We reconnected after more than four decades for a pleasurable conversation.

The bottom line: I loved the games, I enjoyed the writing and I reasoned I could combine the two. The top nearby journalism choices were Indiana University (too big for a small-town kid) and Ball State. It was off to Muncie, Indiana.

Trojan netter

Tom Schuman, East Central number one man, had brilliant first set against the Batesville top seed but fell in the final sets Thursday. His scores were 6-1, 7-6, 6-4. The team lost 5-0 to the Bulldogs.

Staff [Pieratt] photo

A high school tennis form
not to be confused with
any of the all-time greats.

2

CHAPTER 2

Campus Connections

In 1980, Muncie was part of an east central Indiana economy thriving due to the domestic auto industry. The population of 76,000-plus was at an all-time high. Ball State University, founded in 1918 as the Indiana State Normal School Eastern Division, boasted an enrollment of approximately 17,000.

In the early part of the 20th century, Muncie became the new home of five visionaries. The five Ball brothers – Lucius, William, Edmund, Frank and George – were industrialists and philanthropists who moved from New York to Muncie to take advantage of the abundant natural gas supplies and expand their glass container business.

The Balls quickly made their impact in business and on the community. In recognition of the family's generosity, the Indiana General Assembly changed the school's name to Ball Teachers College in 1922 and then Ball State Teachers College in 1929. It eventually became Ball State University (BSU) in 1965.

The sports history at BSU was rather modest at the time I arrived on campus (and university loyalties aside, it has pretty much remained that way). But a few of the highlights:

- Don Shondell, who passed away in late 2021, started the school's men's volleyball program in 1964. He was a tireless advocate in growing the sport nationwide and Ball State became a "cradle of coaches" for both men's and women's programs largely due to his efforts.

Shondell won 769 games in 34 years and took his teams to 13 national tournament Final Fours. The school remained a national power for a few years after his tenure ended, then returned to prominence in 2022, upsetting defending national champion Hawaii twice during the regular season before losing to the Rainbow Warriors in five games in a hotly contested national semifinal.

(Stay tuned for more on that volleyball program).

- Ball State joined the Mid-American Conference (MAC) in 1973. Nine of the current 12 schools are in Ohio (six) and Michigan (three). An early success for BSU came in 1978 with an 8-0 conference football record in a 10-1 season overall. With four shutouts, the Cardinals led the country in scoring defense and ranked third in overall defense. Lineman Ken Kremer went on to a six-year NFL career with the Kansas City Chiefs.

During my four years in Muncie, the football Cards put together a rather forgettable 21-23 record.

- Indiana was and basically still is, first and foremost, a basketball state. And Muncie was one of many high school hotbeds, with the Muncie Central Bearcats collecting nine state titles – with the first coming in 1928.

BSU's only two tournament appearances before my time were in 1957 and 1964 at the NAIA and Division II levels, respectively.

One of the highlights came just before my arrival when the home schedule included longtime rival Indiana State (that's the Larry Bird 33-1 team that lost to Michigan State and Magic Johnson in the national title game), DePaul (led by Mark Aguirre and the third-place finishers in that tournament) and Detroit (post-Dick Vitale but a third-round tourney team with a 22-6 record and future pros Terry Duerod and Earl Cureton).

Ball State defeated Detroit by one point and played single-digit games against Indiana State and DePaul. Friends I met on campus described an electric atmosphere for those big games.

The Cardinals did earn their first (of seven) NCAA tourney berths in 1981. The team was led by 5-foot-9 guard Ray McCallum, a hometown hero who helped produce one of those nine Muncie Central titles in 1979. McCallum, who later returned as the BSU coach for seven seasons and two NCAA tourneys in the 1990s, became the all-time leading conference scorer at the time.

There was no universal television coverage of the tourney in 1981. I vividly recall listening to the radio as the team failed to get the ball to McCallum several times in the closing seconds of a 93-90 loss to fifth-seeded Boston College. The three-point shot was not in place yet, but the ball truly needed to be in McCallum's hands for a chance to pull the upset.

Team Player

Let's go back to the volleyball court and the first of what I call two painful near misses. Sure, they were more painful for those actually playing the games but in these instances the reporter – in these cases me – was close to being part of the team.

While pursuing a journalism degree, a key part of my education was working on the school newspaper. The *Ball State Daily News* was a highly respected publication and many of my collegiate colleagues went on to lengthy and successful media careers.

One of my "beats" was the perennially contending volleyball program. I attended home matches, worked with Shondell and his coaches on reporting the away contests and did a number of feature stories on the players. The setter on the 1982 team, Randy Litchfield, was someone I had met in my initial orientation on campus and who lived in an adjacent dormitory.

The Ohio State University – yes, that one – was the primary volleyball rival for Ball State. A mixture of schools, small and large, comprised the Midwest Intercollegiate Volleyball Association.

I took two eventful trips to Columbus, Ohio in my sophomore year. I traveled with the team the three hours across Interstate 70 and even sat next to the bench to gather as many insights as possible for my stories.

In the regular season matchup, the teams split the first two games. In the crucial game three, I noticed that Ohio State setter Craig Sherman had served out of turn. Sherman was a fiery redhead, so it was not difficult to keep track of his whereabouts on the court.

I mentioned the mix-up to an assistant coach, who protested to the officials. The error cost the Buckeyes two points in a game and match Ball State went on to win. Today, that certainly would have obliterated the line between reporter and participant. But this was college volleyball in 1982.

The team even published a letter to the editor in the campus paper saying, in part, "It is good to know that we have a writer who is knowledgeable of the game and who is not afraid to apply his knowledge. We are happy with the coverage Tom has provided us all season and are hoping we can give him the chance to accompany us to the NCAA finals at Penn State."

To do that required a second victory over Ohio State in the conference tournament final. The Cardinals won the first two games. It would have been a much better

5

story if the team had closed out the match, but Ohio State came back to win the final three games and send Ball State – and me – home on a late-night bus ride wondering what might have been.

Another Ball State volleyball experience was attending, as a spectator, the 1994 NCAA finals in Fort Wayne, Indiana. IPFW (now Purdue Fort Wayne) was another Midwest volleyball power. It was a turning point for the sport as it was the first time in the 25 years of the tournament that a West Coast team had not earned the at-large spot in the final four.

Ball State defeated IPFW in the third-place match. But the bigger news came in the final as Penn State outlasted UCLA 3-2 for the championship. The Bruins had earned 14 of the first 24 NCAA titles, with the other 10 divided among west region powers Pepperdine, Long Beach State, USC and San Diego State.

This match was at a time when teams could only score when they served. While it increased the drama of highly competitive matches, it also produced extremely lengthy battles. That was the case in Fort Wayne with the majority of the crowd rooting for a Nittany Lion upset. A few years later, the sport changed to rally scoring for the benefit of spectators and television audiences.

Cheering on the Cardinals

I noted earlier that the Ball State sports history was rather nondescript at the time of my arrival on campus in 1980. Unfortunately, that has changed little – at least on the national level – since then.

It wasn't due to a lack of support from the Schumans. We actually lived in Muncie during most of the 1990s and became basketball season ticket holders. At various times, we traveled to Detroit, Toledo and Columbus, Ohio for MAC tournaments. The standout player during that time was Bonzi Wells, another local Muncie Central product who became the conference leader in career points (passing Ron Harper of Miami of Ohio) and steals. Wells was a first-round NBA draft choice and averaged 12 points a game over 10 years with five different teams.

For Ball State, it followed its initial 1981 NCAA tournament appearance with a lopsided loss to what was then Memphis State in 1986. Three more first-round losses came against Kansas (by 22 points in 1993), Arizona State (15 points in 1995 during Wells' freshman year) and UCLA (65-57 in 2000).

There were, however, two magical years in the middle of those appearances. Rick Majerus, the popular former assistant to Al McGuire and later head coach at

Marquette, brought his famous appetite and sense of humor to Muncie in 1987. A rather pedestrian 14-14 first season was more focused on bringing some new, tough-minded players into the program. Curtis Kidd and Paris McCurdy were Detroit high school teammates who transferred in from Arkansas Little Rock. At 6-foot-9, 235 pounds, and 6-7, 220, respectively, Kidd and McCurdy brought both physical and mental toughness.

Billy Butts, a star at Muncie North High School, came back home from the University of Michigan. Point guard Scott Nichols was a third Detroit high school product. Two forwards who fit the mold of fundamentally solid Indiana high schoolers were Shawn Parrish (Vincennes) and Greg Miller (Yorktown, just outside Muncie).

Rounding out the key contributors was the wildly athletic Chandler Thompson, a 6-3 forward who propelled Muncie Central to another of its nine high school state titles. The White River in Muncie was a narrow separator of the Central gymnasium from the Ball State campus.

Majerus' second team in 1988-89 began with a 10-0 preseason that included victories over Big 10 teams Minnesota and Purdue. The Boilermakers actually came to the Cards' cozy Irving Gymnasium (give coach Gene Keady credit for benefitting other in-state schools by taking his teams on the road for such contests) and suffered a 14-point defeat in mid-December.

"I'm not afraid to get beat. Fans want to watch these teams play" Keady said, crediting Majerus for his work in turning around the Cardinals. "Coaches should be pulling for each other. I just don't want it (defeats like this) happening to me."

In three previous all-time meetings, Purdue had won by scores of 73-48, 104-77 and 96-47 (one year earlier). Asked after the game what the difference was for the Cardinals from 12 months earlier, Keady said, "A helluva lot of new players."

Majerus, for his part, termed his team "a bunch of misfits" after the upset victory. It was typical for the self-deprecating head coach.

Ball State lost two of its first five conference games, the second a low-scoring contest at home to Toledo on January 18. The Cards would not suffer their next defeat until two months later.

I was working as a sports reporter in Anderson, Indiana at the time and managed to get the assignment covering the MAC tourney in Toledo. At 25-3 entering the event, one would like to think an at-large NCAA bid would be in the offing if necessary. But the team managed to take care of business – barely – with a 77-76 win over Eastern Michigan in the semifinals and 67-65 squeaker over Kent State for the championship.

A school-best No. 9 seed for March Madness was good news. Even better was the fact that the game against No. 8 Pittsburgh would take place in the Midwest Regional at the RCA Dome in Indianapolis (about 60 miles from Muncie). Ball State's 68-64 triumph was its 16th in a row, 29th of the season and first ever in the NCAA tourney. (During the season, the team had also been ranked in the national polls for the first time in school history).

I was a fan at that game, as well as the second-round contest against top-seeded Illinois. There was no shortage of talent on that squad – Kenny Battle, Kendall Gill, Stephen Bardo, Marcus Liberty and Lowell Hamilton – nicknamed the Flying Illini. Ball State surrendered the first 12 points of the game before playing it even the rest of the way in a 72-60 setback. Illinois went on to the Final Four, losing by two points to eventual national champion Michigan.

The danger of a mid-major putting together such a standout season played out as Majerus exited for the head coaching job at Utah. But the core players returned, and assistant Dick Hunsaker was elevated to head coach.

Karen and I had moved to Pensacola, Florida in late 1989, meaning we were in the position of following from afar what was expected to be another standout season. Purdue gained revenge in the season opener with a 14-point home victory. There were also non-conference losses to Indiana State and Memphis State. A 13-3 conference record though, brought a second straight MAC title, followed by a postseason crown – this time at Cobo Hall in Detroit in a homecoming for Kidd, McCurdy and Nichols.

The 24-6 record left the Cardinals with a No. 12 seed and a trip to Salt Lake City, Majerus' new home, for the opening rounds of the NCAA tourney. Up first, No. 5 seed Oregon State and its superstar Gary Payton. Known throughout his long NBA career as a premier trash talker, Payton had little respect for a small school from Indiana that he knew nothing about. It turned out to be his final college game as a three-point play from McCurdy, no slouch as a trash talker, on a short baseline jumper in the final seconds produced a 54-53 Ball State win.

Next was fourth-seeded Louisville, a perennial power with two national titles in the previous decade on its résumé. BSU roared to a big lead in that one, then held on in the battle of Cardinals for a 62-60 victory. Oregon State and Louisville were both ranked in the top 25, but the next test was at an entirely different level – top seed and No. 2-ranked UNLV.

Ball State had its nice mix of talent that had jelled as a team over the past two years. UNLV's starting five was familiar to many fans: forwards Larry Johnson and

8

Stacey Augmon; shooting guard Greg Anthony; point guard Anderson Hunt and center George Ackles. The Rebels, who a week later would defeat Duke by 30 points for the national title, were considered one of the better college teams in the sport's history. I'm a decade into my Ball State fandom and I'm a few thousand miles away in Florida as the biggest game in school history is set to take place in Oakland. Fortunately, the game was scheduled to air on CBS in an era when it was impossible to watch all the tourney contests. Most unfortunately, the first half of the TV doubleheader (a Southeast Region game between Michigan State and Georgia Tech) went into triple overtime.

I was left listening to a scratchy radio signal, losing the broadcast entirely at times, as Ball State battled toe-to-toe with the powerful Rebels. At one point, a Thompson putback dunk over half the other players on the court led announcer Brent Musburger to exclaim: "Oh my! Chandler Thompson, how do you do!"

With the TV broadcast now in place, the game came down to a final possession with Ball State down two. With Nichols out of the game, an errant pass trying to force the ball inside was knocked away and UNLV survived 69-67. The magical journey was over.

In most years, a run like Ball State's would draw the Cinderella label and plenty of attention. But this was also the season of the tragic death of Hank Gathers at Loyola Marymount with his teammate and longtime friend Bo Kimble leading the run-and-gun Lions on their own trip of destiny. Loyola, seeded 11th, was defeated by UNLV 131-101 in the Elite Eight.

With Thompson the lone key returnee in 1991, Ball State finished 21-10 and lost to Cincinnati in the first round of the NIT. The next nine years produced the three first-round losses noted earlier (in 1993, 1995 and 2000). Since then, the Cardinals have rarely advanced to even the semifinals of the MAC tourney.

The biggest highlight, by far, was a visit to the Maui Classic in 2001 and victories over No. 4 Kansas and No. 3 UCLA before a title game loss to top-ranked Duke. The momentum could not be maintained, and the team finished the regular season 19-10. There were three wins in the NIT before a 35-point quarterfinal loss to South Carolina.

Fumbling the Football

On the football field, Ball State often battles on two levels. One, of course,

9

being the opponent on the other side of the field. Second is trying to put fans in the stands. I would help with the latter by attending various games over the years, but the results on both fronts were mixed. At one point, in order to try and meet NCAA attendance requirements, tickets were being sold for $2.

Off the sidelines, I mentioned the standout season in 1978. The next 30 years did result in four bowl games – all losses. The breakdown:

- Fresno State, 27-6, in the 1989 California Bowl
- Utah State, 42-33, in the 1993 Las Vegas Bowl
- Nevada, 18-15, in the 1996 Vegas Bowl
- Rutgers, 52-30 in the January 2008 International Bowl

Karen and I took our 5-year-old daughter to Las Vegas in 1996. What stood out? Not much from the game. I played blackjack at the same table the night before with ESPN analyst (and former college coach) Mike Gottfried. There was a non-stop flow of airplanes heading over Sam Boyd Stadium (west of Sin City) during the game. It was cold in mid-December with even a few snow flurries. And we struggled to keep up with 5-year-old Megan as she dashed her way around McCarron International Airport before our redeye flight back to Indiana.

But the 2008 football season mirrored the 1988-1990 two-year basketball run. A powerful offense and an opportunistic defense produced 12 consecutive victories, all but one by double digits. There was national TV attention (five games on the ESPN networks) and relatively big crowds (more than 20,000 for four of the six home games).

Game four of the season was a 42-20 victory under the lights at Indiana University's Memorial Stadium in Bloomington. Steve Nall, my longtime friend from Anderson, and I were among more than 41,000 fans in attendance. It was Ball State's first win ever over a Bowl Championship Series school. Star running back MiQuale Lewis ran for 166 yards and four touchdowns on the way to 1,736 and 22, respectively, in those categories for the season.

The celebration was muted, however, by the loss of leading receiver Dante Love, who entered the game leading the nation at 144.3 yards per game. Hit near the sideline after catching a short pass, Love suffered a cervical spine fracture and spinal cord injury. His playing career was over, but he remained an inspirational leader for the remainder of the season.

Twelve wins meant a trip to the MAC Championship game at Ford Field in Detroit against East Division champion Buffalo. I made the trip north from Indianapolis with Steve and two other friends. The teams had not played during the regular season. Fans, however, were counting on a win with widespread speculation about a possible bowl matchup against established small school power Boise State.

Food poisoning the night before the game for QB Nate Davis (nearly 3,600 yards and 26 touchdowns on the season) didn't help. Neither did four fumbles, including two that were returned for 92 and 74-yard touchdowns. A 42-24 loss was the result.

While dreams of a bigger bowl and a more high-profile opponent were dashed, 12-1 does get a team into the postseason The BSU destination was Mobile, Alabama in January 2009 and a matchup against the Tulsa Golden Hurricane. Steve and I headed south.

Ten days after the conference title loss, head coach Brady Hoke resigned for the same position at San Diego State. Two years later, he was the head man at Michigan. Hoke was replaced by offensive coordinator Stan Parrish, who won two of 33 games during his most recent head coaching stint over 20 years earlier at Kansas State.

The opponent nickname in Mobile was appropriate for two reasons. The speed on offense for the Golden Hurricane was too much for the Cardinal defense to handle from the opening kickoff. Tulsa led 24-13 at the half but had dominated the contest. Then Mother Nature took over with swirling winds and sideways rain that lasted the remainder of the game. Tulsa did all the scoring in the second half in a 45-13 final.

What a roller coaster ride for the Cardinals and their fans (I attended half of the 14 games that season). But even though it was a disappointing finish, the "highs" were certainly more welcome than the general mediocrity that existed. Parrish went 6-19 the next two years before being fired.

(Side note: More than 13 years later, while in New Orleans for the 2022 Final Four, we ran into star tight end Darius Hill. He spotted Steve's Ball State shirt and we reminisced about that special season).

Worst and Best of Times

The next bowl opportunity for Ball State came after the 2012 season. It was a matchup with Central Florida in the infamous Beef 'O' Brady's Bowl in St. Petersburgh, Florida. It just so happened that the Schuman family was scheduled to take a holiday cruise leaving out of nearby Tampa two days later.

So, we adjusted our travel plans and arrived in an unseasonably cold Florida.

While tailgating outside in the brisk conditions prior to going inside the dome for the game, I was interviewed by a local newspaper reporter and asked whether I thought the chilly conditions would benefit the Cardinals. That rather absurd question unfortunately proved to be one of the highlights of the night.

Central Florida quarterback Blake Bortles (drafted third overall by Jacksonville two years later) completed two early TD passes as the Golden Knights rolled to a 38-17 victory. It was Ball State's fifth loss in as many bowl appearances, with a 23-20 setback to Arkansas State in the January 2014 GoDaddy Bowl extending that streak to six.

My family claimed the St. Petersburgh trip was one of the longest nights of their lives, but I made a major comeback by taking them to Disney World the next day. The cool conditions kept the crowds down and we enjoyed a memorable time in the self-proclaimed "happiest place on earth."

I continued to make the occasional trips to Muncie to watch the Cardinals and followed other games on television or the radio. The latter two were the only options during the shortened 2020 COVID season.

Ball State opened on November 4 at Miami, Ohio with an ill-timed screen pass resulting in an interception and a 38-31 defeat. What followed was seven consecutive high-scoring wins, primarily close games in which the Cardinals prevailed after a tradition of finding a way to lose such contests.

The MAC title game delivered revenge from 12 years earlier with a 38-28 defeat of favored Buffalo. A 28-point second quarter paved the way to an Arizona Bowl berth against No. 22 San Jose State of the Mountain West Conference.

You can be assured I would have made the trip to Tucson, Arizona in hope of that long-awaited bowl triumph. But COVID was still the name of the game, and no fans were allowed. CBS provided the coverage as I watched Ball State roll up 27 points in a near perfect first quarter in a 34-13 triumph.

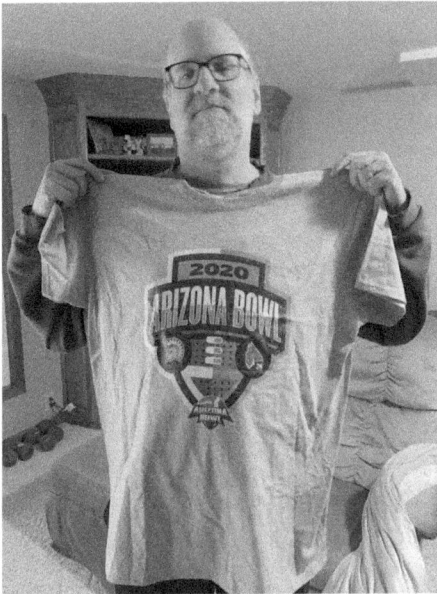

Prepping for the 2020 Arizona Bowl, which would become Ball State's long-awaited first – and only – Division I postseason win.

On the road to see the Cardinals at Wyoming in 2021.

CHAPTER 3

Making It a Career

The trip down the bumpy Ball State memory lane started with my reporter role covering the volleyball team for the campus newspaper. After graduation in 1984, it was time to embark on a career that began with both newspapers and sports. The experiences over the next six years were varied and memorable.

Watseka, Illinois

It started in Watseka, Illinois and the *Iroquois County Times-Republic,* a five-day afternoon newspaper. I was the sports editor on a three-person editorial staff, striving to provide coverage of sports at 10 high schools in addition to other community programs.

Watseka was located on U.S. 24, northwest of West Lafayette and Purdue University and 30 miles south of Kankakee, Illinois. Of the 10 high schools, I recall four of them having fewer than 100 students. They ranged geographically from Central High School in Clifton (near Kankakee) to Milford and Wellington in the southern part of the county.

Milford was memorable for its carpeted basketball floor. The reason for that distinction was that the space doubled as an activity center during the school day. Wellington was the smallest of the small schools with 56 students. The story I have told many times over the years is that you could account for just about everyone of those 56 at a boys' basketball game – from the players, managers and cheerleaders to pep band and concession workers.

In addition to Watseka, other schools (most remain; several have succumbed to consolidation) were Cissna Park, Crescent City, Iroquois West, Donovan, Sheldon and Buckley-Loda. The games came at me fast and furious. I often took photos and kept statistics at the same time before preparing both the images and stories for publication.

Watseka possessed a strong basketball program. One of its main rivals was the Hoopeston-East Lynn Cornjerkers (you can't make these names up). After Watseka was eliminated from tournament play in the 1984-85 season, I followed the undefeated Cornjerkers and their star player in floppy-haired senior guard Thad Matta. Hoopeston finished third in the state tournament, losing to eventual state champion Providence St. Mel and its star player Lowell Hamilton (who four years later was on the Illinois team that defeated Ball State in the NCAA tourney).

Matta played collegiately at Southern Illinois and Butler before beginning a lengthy career on the sidelines with head coaching stops at Butler, Xavier and Ohio State. More than 30 years after that season, I met Matta and a mutual friend at an Indianapolis restaurant for lunch. I shared with him newspaper stories and memories from that special Hoopeston season, and he provided insights about college basketball and the business behind the games.

One of the more fascinating interviews I was able to conduct outside of the high school space was with Indiana basketball legend Rick Mount. Then 38 years old, Mount was a guest at Watseka's summer basketball camp. While he talked to the 60-plus campers in attendance on proper shooting techniques, he also sank 18 of 20 long-range jumpers.

A portion of Mount's résumé as one of the greatest pure shooters the game has known: Scoring averages of 20.4, 23.6, 33.1 and 33.1 in four seasons at Lebanon High School. In the era before the three-point shot, his three varsity campaigns at Purdue generated 28.4, 33.3 and 35.4 averages. He teamed with backcourt mate Billy Keller to lead the Boilers to an NCAA runner-up finish to UCLA in 1969.

Mount, who was the first high school athlete to appear on the cover of *Sports Illustrated*, played six years in the American Basketball Association, including on one championship team.

"I went to the pros and played well but had some injuries and problems with coaches trying to turn me into a passer," Mount said in that Watseka interview. *"Once you start playing for money, the rah-rah goes out of it."*

Wabash, Indiana

Have we mentioned that Indiana is a basketball state? And Indianapolis Colts quarterback Peyton Manning was later credited with generating widespread football interest with his outstanding play and personality over 13 seasons.

But Wabash, Indiana is baseball country. I arrived in Wabash in late 1985 as sports editor of the *Plain Dealer* newspaper. This time, there were four primary high schools in the county – Wabash, Northfield, Southwood and Manchester – although we'll touch on another interesting educational institution in a moment. Manchester College was also a focus of the sports coverage.

In a few magical months of 1986, here is what happened on the baseball diamond:

High school baseball had been dominated for years by the likes of LaPorte, Logansport and other large schools. In 1986, Wabash possessed one star, a cast of fundamentally sound players and a savvy coach. It advanced through the state tournament to the final at Bush Stadium (home of the AAA Indianapolis Indians).

The opponent in the championship game was Marion, located about 20 miles south of Wabash on State Road 15. The joke at the time was the game could have been played in an open field in La Fontaine – a town of about 875 people located midway between the two.

It was a David vs. Goliath matchup, and not only because Marion was approximately three times the size of its northeastern Indiana neighbor.

Marion, like the Muncie Central program that produced top players for Ball State, was basketball royalty. The Giants were in the middle of three consecutive state hoops championships, led by co-Mr. Basketball and future Indiana University guards Jay Edwards and Lyndon Jones. The school had also won the state baseball title two years earlier. Wabash's two state team titles in school history had come in wrestling in the 1920s.

It was, from the outside, the big city bully against the little country kid hoping to get a chance to play on the main field. But, of course, that was not the way the Wabash team approached the contest. It had, in fact, defeated the Giants early in the season as a part of a 12-game winning streak.

The Wabash star was Keith Shepherd, a strapping right-handed pitcher with enough talent that he signed his professional contract with the Pittsburgh Pirates (he was drafted a few weeks prior) while sitting in the dugout following the title game.

Shepherd played professionally for 11 seasons, including parts of four years in the majors with the Phillies, Rockies, Red Sox and Orioles. He earned two wins and three saves while on the mound.

While Shepherd gained much of the attention, No. 2 pitcher Tom Dempsey (I always thought of the New Orleans Saints field goal kicker when covering this Dempsey in his various sports) was a star in his own right. He entered the final with a 15-0 record and 0.82 ERA in 96 innings. On this day, he gave up a run in the first inning but didn't allow another Giants runner to reach scoring position. He struck out 12, walked two and only surrendered a pair of first-inning hits.

The Marion pitcher was Eric Persinger, a starter on the powerful Giants basketball teams. He matched Dempsey, shutting out Wabash until the top of the seventh and final inning. A two-out single brought in the tying run and, one out later, light-hitting catcher Brent Johnson (.155 average) flared a ball near the foul line in right for the go-ahead score. Dempsey retired the side in order in the bottom of the inning and the celebration was on.

In a *Plain Dealer* story 30 years later, Johnson recalled the magical season.

"There's no reason we should have been where we were with the level of talent that we beat," he said. "We were a lot of average high school baseball players, but I truly believe that because of the coaching that we had and what Coach (Chris) Rood was able to instill in us and the program he had built, it was designed to take average ball players ... and extract more than you could ever imagine from them."

As for the title game, "I know I was always a bundle of nerves," Johnson added. "I remember sitting there before the game and I was very nervous. Coach Rood could tell, and I remember it very vividly. He just came and sat beside me and said, 'Hey man, what's wrong?' And I said, 'I'm just really nervous.' He said 'Listen, don't be. This is worth everything we've done. This is the icing on the cake and no matter what happens, just enjoy what we've been doing and try to have fun out there.' That's what we did."

Rood was a history teacher at the high school and baseball coach from 1971-94. The baseball field was renamed a year later to honor him after an early death. He simply loved the game of baseball and teaching – whether it was in the classroom or on the field.

The celebration of the state title started in Indianapolis and continued back home with fans young and old. I recall Mayor Dallas Winchester keeping his promise to let the players shave his head if they brought home the championship.

While the high schoolers were wrapping up their season in late June, Wabash's top youth players were gearing up for a tourney run of their own. This is the annual spectacle for 11- and 12-year-olds across the country and world that culminates in the highly publicized Little League World Series in Williamsport, Pennsylvania. Wabash High School defeated the Giants for their title. In Little League baseball in the 1980s, Wabash was the "giants" with a record seven consecutive state tournament appearances. Getting to that Final Four each year was an achievement in itself. In 1986, that included two close Section wins against Fort Wayne St. Joseph – 3-1 in nine innings in the preliminaries and 3-2 in the final.

South Bend East Side was the primary foe in the state tourney. Wabash earned 4-3 and 7-3 wins for its second title in four years. Next up, one step short of Williamsport, was the Great Lakes region championship in Bradley-Bourbonnais, Illinois (about 30 miles north of where I had started my career in Watseka).

With baseball fever in full swing in mid-August, the staff photographer for the *Plain Dealer* and I became road warriors. We made the approximate 2½-hour drive to Illinois to cover each day's game, returning home to prepare the stories and photos for the next day's publication. That routine continued for three days in dominating victories (outscoring state champions from Ohio, Michigan and Illinois by a 22-3 total).

Flashback: Four years earlier, I was one game (in a best-of-five volleyball match) away from covering the Ball State volleyball team in the NCAA Final Four in State College, Pennsylvania. Now, it was one more six-inning win, and we would be off to Williamsport in the Keystone State.

It wasn't meant to be, however, as Norridge, Illinois recorded 6-2 and 2-0 wins over the Wabash team. Near miss No. 2.

Still, it was quite a summer of baseball in Wabash.

Legendary Figure

I hinted at an educational facility in Wabash County in addition to the traditional schools. That was White's Institute, a faith-based program for at-risk teenagers. It was not the place where one would expect to find one of Indiana and the country's most outstanding basketball players at all levels.

Clyde Lovellette was a giant man in both size (listed at 6-foot-9 but appearing to be even taller) and impact. Some of his on-court achievements included:
- Two-time All-State performer at Terre Haute Garfield High School. In his junior year, the team won 31 straight games before losing in the state final to Shelbyville.
- Two-time All-American at the University of Kansas, leading the nation in

scoring as a senior with 28.4 points per game. Playing for legendary coach Phog Allen, the Jayhawks won the 1951-52 NCAA championship. Lovellette had 33 points and 17 rebounds in the title victory over St. John's.

- Leading scorer of the 1952 Olympic team that won its first seven games by an average of 20 points before defeating Russia for the gold medal.
- Three NBA championships in an 11-year career in which he averaged 17 points and 9.3 rebounds. In a precursor of today's game, he was one of the first big men to move away from the basket. He used a one-handed set shot and was able to play both forward positions in addition to center.

Very few of the young men and women at White's likely knew about Lovellette's storied past. Yes, he coached some basketball while there, but his primary mission was to help these troubled teens get their lives back on track and he eventually served as director of White's vocational and educational programs. Lovellette took that role seriously and he was successful at it – and was remembered as much for his off-court heroics as his basketball ones when he died in 2016.

A fun story in Watseka in 1985 with Rick Mount, one of the greatest basketball shooters of all time.

A ball from the state championship baseball team at Wabash High School in 1986.

CHAPTER 4

Indians and a Whole Lot More

ollowing more than two years in Wabash, I moved on to a third sports position – this one as part of a three-person department in Anderson, Indiana. Among the additional opportunities in Anderson were Big Ten basketball (covering both Indiana and Purdue games) and professional sports (the Indianapolis Colts were conducting training camp in Anderson, and both the Colts and Indiana Pacers were about 35 miles away in the state capital).

The Anderson journey starts, however, with high school basketball. The city boasted three schools at the time in Anderson, Highland and Madison Heights. The Anderson High School Athletic and Education Building, forever known as the Wigwam, (capacity 8,996) boasted the longest tradition. An elaborate dance with a boy and girl in Indian dress was the centerpiece of the pregame ceremony. Sellout crowds were common and Indians tickets were subject to "custody" proceedings in divorce cases.

Anderson was part of the North Central Conference (NCC), a collection of basketball powers in primarily industrial cities across a large swath of the state. The aforementioned Muncie Central and Marion were longtime members of the NCC as were Richmond, New Castle, Kokomo, Lafayette Jefferson and Logansport. It was not unusual for two or three conference teams to advance to the four-team state finals.

(Side note: Indiana possessed nine of the 10 largest high school gymnasiums in the world at the time, led by the 9,325-seat Chrysler Fieldhouse in New Castle).

There was no shortage of star players at the three Anderson schools, both

20

historically and in the late 1980s. When I arrived, each school was led by a Hall of Fame coach with vastly different demeanors.

The fiery Norm Held went 343-114 at Anderson in 18 years with four state runner-up finishes. His 31-year career included more than 500 victories. He coached two Mr. Basketball award winners – Troy Lewis and Kojak Fuller.

Alan Darner, conservative in his demeanor and public expectations for his teams, recorded a 142-59 record at Highland in 10 seasons. He later won two state titles at Pike High School in Indianapolis. Darner's two sons, Linc and Tige, were Indiana All-Stars while playing for the Scots.

Phil Buck was closing out his long playing and coaching career at Madison Heights, where he won nine sectional titles. Buck (495 career victories) had been inducted into the Hall of Fame five years earlier. A beloved mentor to so many in the game, Buck was so impressed by the fact that my wife, Karen, would come to the games and help me record statistics that he would send over a box of popcorn for her to enjoy.

The three Anderson schools combined to dominate the Wigwam-based sectional. The field in the historical single-class system included Madison County neighbors Alexandria, Pendleton Heights, Lapel and Elwood as well as nearby Daleville.

Madison Heights, led by 5-foot-7 dynamo Milan Stubblefield, won its second straight sectional in my first year in 1988. A year later, Alexandria ended a 26-year sectional drought by claiming the title. Although the Tigers would win a state crown nine years later in the first year of the class system, any longtime Alexandria fan would say they treasured a sectional victory at the Wigwam more than any other achievement.

Boiler Up

Three months into my time at the *Herald Bulletin*, I had the opportunity to cover the Purdue basketball team as it advanced to the second weekend of the NCAA tournament at the Silverdome in Pontiac, Michigan.

It was a star-studded field but one the Boilermakers were expected to conquer. The top seed in the Midwest Regional entered with a 29-3 record and a 29-point victory earlier in the season over Sweet 16 opponent Kansas State. It was the senior swan song for the Triplets – forward Todd Mitchell, point guard Everette Stephens and shooting guard Troy Lewis.

Yes, the same Lewis who four years earlier averaged 35.3 points as a senior at

Anderson and shared the Mr. Basketball award with Delray Brooks of Michigan City Rogers. Lewis scored more than 2,000 points in his collegiate career and was a two-time all-Big Ten selection.

Kansas State was led by future NBA star Mitch Richmond. The other two entries were Vanderbilt (center Will Perdue was its top player) and Kansas (which had lost 11 games during the regular season). The Jayhawks were led by senior Danny Manning.

Purdue could not stop Richmond (27 points and 11 rebounds) and crucial mistakes on offense produced a 73-70 setback. Lewis scored 19 points in his final college game.

Lewis said at the time: *"It seemed like we just could not get our shots to go in and it seemed like everything they threw up went in."*

Kansas, the eighth seed in the region, put up 13-point wins over both Vanderbilt and Kansas State, then returned "home" to Kansas City for the Final Four. It avenged losses to Duke and Oklahoma to claim the national title in what became known as "Danny and the Miracles."

Keady, for his part after the upset loss: *"My hat's off to Kansas State. Even though we had a great season, it was a team that was better than us tonight."*

To some, Keady played second fiddle to the Indiana Hoosiers and coach Bobby Knight. But I always admired Keady's no-nonsense approach and straightforward dealings with the media. He was willing to play anybody anywhere and rarely made excuses when his team fell short. Nearly all would agree that he has been one of the good guys in the game.

The public opinions on Knight, of course, encompassed a much larger range. The intention here is not to debate the accomplishments or shortcomings of the Hall of Fame coach. But there are a few interactions I had that do stand out.

- A story I have retold often over the years involved a heavily favored Indiana team playing a very poor first half at home at Assembly Hall against Minnesota. At halftime, Knight refused to allow the players into the locker room, saying afterward that they had done nothing in the first 20 minutes that deserved a seat during the break. Indiana came back to win the game.
- Big Monday was an ESPN creation that featured 9:30 p.m. Eastern time starts for two conference teams (following a Big East game earlier in the evening). In 1989, I reported on a 104-89 Big Monday win against Iowa. It followed earlier one-point wins in late night contests at Purdue and Michigan State.

I captured this Knight tirade following the game:

"This is the last Monday night game at 9:30 I hope Indiana ever plays. They've talked in this league about exposure. We don't want any more exposure."

"We don't need this anymore. We're just going to tell them and, in fact, I think we may be told by our Athletic Committee that that's it for us, playing 9:30 games."

"They're tired of it, our kids are tired of it; we're all tired of it."

"I think it will be a magnanimous gesture on our part when we say the rest of you can have that exposure – take our spot and expose yourself in any way you want to."

No matter your feelings about Knight and the Hoosiers, it was never boring in Bloomington.

Going Professional

Professional sports had not been part of my reporting experience as of 1988. But the local fan support of the Indianapolis Colts was only exacerbated by the fact that the team spent a portion of its summer training camp utilizing the facilities at Anderson University.

Small colleges were and sometimes still are a popular destination for NFL franchises. Sure, they get to take over the football fields, dorms and other campus amenities. And it's a great way to expand the fan base. But one of the other key factors is teams want a location where their players will hopefully stay out of trouble; in other words, the less there is to do in a community the better.

That didn't stop a few local bars from becoming frequent destinations for players looking to escape after the practices, meetings, lifting weights and other activities of a training camp day. Our news staff was put to work a few times with police reports involving players who let off a little too much steam.

On the field, practices could be rather repetitious and uneventful to the untrained eye. I sometimes drifted over to one of the auxiliary fields where punter Rohn Stark and placekicker Dean Biasucci, both veterans, put in their work but also enjoyed a great deal of leisure time. Kickers have the luxury of not participating in many of the typical drills, leaving more opportunities to connect with the fans.

While the Colts later enjoyed two decades of stability at the quarterback position with Peyton Manning and Andrew Luck, that was far from the case in the late 1980s. Gary Hogeboom, a nine-year veteran, had been injured four times since Indianapolis acquired him from Dallas in 1986.

Jack Trudeau, drafted by the Colts out of Illinois in the second round in 1986, ended up starting 19 games in his first two years. Add in Chris Chandler, a third-round selection from Washington in 1988.

Hogeboom expected to return to his starting role. I was in the Colts locker room at their Indianapolis complex when he found out that wasn't going to be the case after a season-opening overtime loss to the Houston Oilers.

Coach Ron Meyer announced the following: *"Gary Hogeboom will be demoted, and Chris Chandler will be moved up (to second string) and get more and more action."*

A portion of Hogeboom's reaction: *"I told him to cut me, immediately. I guess the reason was, I haven't produced ... I've had a hard time holding up in the games.*

"Right now, I'm still with the Colts. I don't know what's going on. It's a tough business. I've done everything I can to work with Ron and the staff. I've gone over it a lot. There are other things to do in life. I want to be released or cut."

Trudeau lasted two games before being injured with Chandler starting the final 13 contests. Hogeboom was on the move after the season, ending up in Arizona.

The biggest moment on the field came on October 31 in the first-ever Monday Night Football game in Indianapolis. Fans were provided masks of ABC announcers Al Michaels, Frank Gifford and Dan Dierdorf in what was the noisiest Hoosier Dome atmosphere to that point.

Eric Dickerson, acquired from the Los Angeles Rams exactly one year earlier, gave the fans plenty to cheer about with four touchdowns and 159 yards. His three first-quarter scores produced a 21-0 lead on the way to a 45-10 halftime count and eventual 55-23 victory.

A personal significance is this was the first event in which I and the *Herald Bulletin* transmitted a story back to the office remotely. I recall a rather large computer with both ends of a landline phone being placed into couplers in order to hopefully make the connection. It could be an arduous and often frustrating process but an important step forward in newspaper technology.

My sports writing experiences took a southern detour in the fall of 1989 and spring of 1990. Karen (we were married in 1987) received an exciting job opportunity in Pensacola, Florida. I worked several jobs during our time there, including as a writer with the *Pensacola News Journal*.

The Panhandle is football and baseball country. In the fall, I covered various high school sporting events and wrote some feature stories. As the Washington High School football team prepared for a state semifinal game against powerhouse Manatee of Bradenton, I interviewed a sophomore safety who was one of the defensive leaders.

He was soft spoken at the time, but later became a vocal leader as a linebacker with the Florida State Seminoles and Tampa Bay Buccaneers. Considered one of the best players ever at this position and a winner of the prestigious Walter Payton NFL Man of the Year award, he was future Hall of Famer Derrick Brooks.

In the first week of January, I was assigned a baseball season preview. I visited one of the city's top teams at Tate High School and it was easy to see why so many eventual major leaguers come from the Sunshine State. The field was in pristine condition and the squad was preparing to open its season in just a few weeks. In Indiana, baseball teams are fortunate if they get outdoors in late March and the approximate six-week season often involves dodging spring rainstorms.

Indiana once had nine of the 10 largest high school basketball gyms in the world, led by Chrysler Fieldhouse in New Castle.

CHAPTER 5

Back in the Hoosier State

█████ everal factors led us to return to Indiana in 1990. While my sports position at the *Herald Bulletin* was no longer available, I was fortunate to be hired as a correspondent and provided a wonderful opportunity that focused on a local connection to the Indianapolis Motor Speedway (IMS).

Anderson businessman Jeff Stoops was a very successful trucking company owner and later Freightliner dealer who also owned a winning sprint car team. Stoops' dream was to build that operation into a starting spot in what Hoosiers (and much of the world) know as the "Greatest Spectacle in Racing."

In those days, the famous month of May was indeed a full month. Seven hours of available practice time Monday through Friday and four days of qualifications all led to the Memorial Day weekend spectacular. The Indianapolis 500 was, and still is, the largest single day sporting event in the world with as many as an estimated 350,000 people converging at 16th Street and Georgetown Roads in what is officially Speedway, Indiana.

Auto racing, no matter the form it takes, is an expensive proposition today. It was the same in the early 1990s. I wrote a column outlining some of the common expenditures at that time. A few of the key items:

- *Race car: A rolling chassis (car with suspension and steering system) listed for $200,000 in 1989. Superspeedway kits, at $30,000 each, are needed to help set up the car for those events.*
- *Engine: Plan $60,000 to $80,000 per engine with eight to 10 engines per race car for the year. Indy-car racing engines must be rebuilt every 500 to 600 miles*

at an average cost of $10,000 to $12,000 per rebuild.

- Wheels: The rolling chassis comes with four wheels. For the season, plan to have a dozen more sets of wheels (48 wheels) at $1,200 per wheel.
- Tires: Rules allow 44 tires for the 500-mile events. The cost is $600 to $700 per set.
- Fuel: An Indy car gets 1.8 miles per gallon. A team may use as much as 40,000 gallons during the month of May.
- Transporter: These rolling machine shops complete with spare parts and more cost between $175,000 and $300,000.
- Spare parts: For the year, allow at least $200,000 for disposable parts and another $30,000 to $50,000 for gearbox parts.
- Team costs: Varies greatly but one must allow for salaries for drivers, engineers, fabricators, crew, office employees and truck drivers, along with travel costs, lodging, rental cars and food allowances.

According to Championship Auto Racing Teams, the cost of operating a top-flight, competitive Indy-car team for a season averages $1,100 per mile. That compares to 61 cents per mile for the average motorist.

The Stoops' car was driven by Steve Butler of Kokomo, Indiana, the three-time defending United States Auto Club sprint

The Stoops racing team includes (from left) co-owner Jeff Stoops, driver Steve Butler and co-owner Teri Stoops.

Stoops' enjoy speedy start

By TOM SCHUMAN
H-B sports writer

The Anderson-based Stoops Racing team is off to a fast start in preparations for the Indianapolis 500.

The Stoops team, including owners Jeff and Teri Stoops, was the first on the track when testing opened at the Speedway last Wednesday. The 1987 Lola, driven by Kokomo's Steve Butler, reached 196.6 mph.

"We're probably as tickled as we could be for the first day," Jeff Stoops said of the first venture at the Speedway for the new Indy-car team. "We're pretty excited we got up to speed right away. We're feeling pretty good at this point."

Butler, the three-time defending USAC sprint car champion, received help on his opening Indy-car ride from veteran Johnny Rutherford. Chris Paulsen, chief mechanic for the Stoops' team, has worked with Rutherford in the past.

"We tried to schedule two days with J.R.," Stoops said, "but we had to cancel Thursday. (Weather conditions also kept the team off the track Friday and Monday). "He spent a lot of time just driving around the Speedway with Steve in a passenger car."

Butler ran 65 laps in the Lola, attempting to work up to full speed in about 25 of those laps. A driver must exceed 195 mph in 10 consecutive laps as part of the rookie orientation April 27-29.

"We had no problems at all (with the car)," said Stoops, who added the team hoped to reach 200 mph in the next testing session.

The weatherman plays a major role in setting up testing dates for all the Indy-car teams. Stoops said the Speedway is "pretty solidly booked" for the rest of March and April, with the trick being that reservations must be confirmed by 3 p.m. the previous day.

The $3,000-a-day fee — covering the cost of safety crews and medical teams — must be paid if the track is booked. Thus, a sunny forecast at 3 p.m. Monday could prove costly if there is a thunderstorm on Tuesday. Up to three teams are allowed to test at the same time, however, with the fee split between them.

Stoops has several days booked in the coming weeks, and is also hoping to acquire additional time on the track for Butler.

There are currently 36 entrants for the May 28 race.

Owners Jeff and Teri Stoops of Anderson, Indiana, did their best to qualify a car for the Indianapolis 500.

car champion. Johnny Rutherford, winner of three Indianapolis 500s (1974, 1976 and 1980) served as a driver consultant. Chief mechanic Chris Paulsen had worked with Rutherford, among others, in his career.

Early testing proved promising, and Butler led the way in rookie orientation. But in the week leading up to qualifying, a blown engine came first. That was followed by a crash in which Butler suffered a broken collarbone. A 1988 Lola was purchased from A.J. Foyt Racing, but time was lost due to rain and the team was unable to get the car up to speed for an initial qualifying attempt.

The misfortune continued into the second week. Even with the veteran Rutherford getting behind the wheel, Stoops Racing was unable to qualify. A similar scenario played out the following year with a mixture of promising developments followed by ultimate disappointment. In the end, there were no regrets as all involved worked hard and did their best.

Stoops, Butler, Paulsen and others were most patient and accommodating with their time for this reporter. It was a most enjoyable experience to be almost embedded with the team in their quest – no matter the outcome.

Side note: For many years, the Indianapolis Motor Speedway was basically in use only during the month of May. That changed in 1994 when the Brickyard 400 debuted. Karen and I attended the first 17 of these races. And even though the track was/is too flat for optimum NASCAR racing, it was always memorable to be part of such a major community event.

The Speedway also opened its doors to its Indianapolis neighbors. At various times, I walked (fundraiser), ran (half marathon associated with the Indy 500), bicycled and drove my car (Brickyard 400 activities) around the 2½-mile racing surface. When COVID rammed its way into all our lives like an unforgiving wall in one of the Speedway turns, Karen and I even received our first vaccine in the IMS garages as part of a drive through public health program that served as many as 4,000 people in one day.

While spending numerous days in May at IMS, at times I would travel the few miles down 16th Street to cover an Indianapolis Indians game that night at Bush Stadium (site of the 1986 Wabash state title game). The AAA squad that began play in 1902 earned four consecutive American Association titles at one point. Several of those teams were led by local legend Razor Shines, a first baseman who totaled 15 hits in parts of four seasons with the parent Montreal Expos. He spent most of nine years with the Indians.

Earl and Lou

Two other highlights from the Anderson sports writing days were talking to a pair of sports figures – unassuming in their appearance – who were at the top of their professions.

A crew cut and plastic-framed glasses led fellow competitors to call him "Square Earl." Bowling observers called Earl Anthony a champion and one of the two men (along with Dick Weber) who vaulted the sport to unprecedented popularity.

Anthony was coming to Anderson for a fund-raising breakfast and clinic for a non-profit that served children with special needs. I spoke with him to preview that appearance and recap his illustrious career.

After his minor league baseball career was cut short by injury, Anthony worked in a grocery warehouse (sounds like Kurt Warner 30 years before the Hall of Fame quarterback rose to fame). He practiced his bowling and joined the tour in 1963 but quit after three events.

Success followed after rejoining the tour in 1970. He overcame a divorce and heart attack in 1978 but abruptly retired while still at the top of his game in 1983 at age 45. Anthony won 43 Professional Bowling Association titles, six PBA Championships and is a member of the PBA and American Bowling Congress halls of fame.

Anthony said he typically bowled more than 300 games a week. The toll was more mental than physical.

"I looked forward to bowling every day," he recalled. *"Even if a tourney ended on Saturday, I couldn't wait until the next one started on Monday."*

"In 1982, there was a major change in my attitude. I couldn't wait for the tournament to end. It's difficult to explain. The lack of privacy and traveling had something to do with it but mostly it's that mental attitude."

Despite being told he would never bowl again after his heart attack, Anthony was determined to return. He finally received the go-ahead to resume a light schedule.

"They (doctors) told me I could start bowling the next day. They said I could bowl three or four frames and go for a short walk," he shared. Not one used to sitting around, Anthony said, *"I went and bowled four games, ran a half mile and walked a half mile. In two weeks, I intended to bowl the Waukegan Open, where I was the defending champion. I did and finished third."*

Anthony later won seven titles on the PBA Senior Tour to give him 50 for his career. He died of injuries from a fall at age 63.

In September 1988, I covered what was then an annual football rivalry between Notre Dame and Purdue. Fighting Irish Coach Lou Holtz, 13-10 in his first two seasons in South Bend, saw his team score 42 first half points that day on the way to a 52-7 triumph. The team moved to 3-0 with earlier victories over Big Ten rivals Michigan and Michigan State.

Holtz, one of the great motivators of his time who made a living out of managing expectations, declared the following after the rout.

"We're awful young if you really look at it. It's difficult to be ready each week, which you have to be with our schedule. I have no idea (how good we are). We still have a long way to go."

The Irish were indeed young. The two touchdown passes against the Boilermakers were the second and third of junior quarterback Tony Rice's career. Rocket Ismail and future NFL running back Ricky Watters were two of the primary receivers. Tackle Chris Zorich and linebacker Michael Stonebreaker were key defenders.

Notre Dame grew up in a hurry, defeating then No. 1 Miami (winners of 36 straight in the regular season and having outscored the Irish 133-20 in four recent contests) 31-30 in the famous Catholics vs. Convicts game. It closed the regular season with a win at No. 2 USC and earned the school's 11th national title with a 34-21 defeat of West Virginia in the Fiesta Bowl.

I had a one-on-one interview with Holtz two years earlier when he visited Wabash for a speaking engagement. He was the same animated, energetic person who guided six different programs to bowl games over 29 seasons and worked as a studio analyst for ESPN.

CHAPTER 6

Hoops Heaven

fter returning to Anderson from Florida and performing the Indianapolis 500/Indianapolis Indians double as a correspondent in the spring of 1990, I left the day-to-day world of sports reporting. I became a news editor and later assist managing editor and managing editor of the *Herald Bulletin*.

But there would be one more major sports writing experience. Anderson, for all its basketball passion and success, had not earned a state title since 1946 (a team led by future Harlem Globetrotter Jumpin' Johnny Wilson, who was a volunteer coach for this squad). The 1996-97 Indians entered the season with the goal of ending that 51-year drought.

As managing editor, I teamed with graphics editor and good friend Phil Miller (a Ball State graduate a year before I and colleague at the *Herald Bulletin*) to do our own "Season on the Brink" to capture what was a hoped-for magical season.

The real *Season on the Brink*, of course, was John Feinstein's 1986 book that went behind the scenes of the Indiana University basketball team in 1985-86 under the guidance of Knight. The coach gave the extremely talented author unparalleled access, which produced a highly popular – and somewhat controversial – look inside the program.

We didn't claim to have Feinstein's abilities. But what he had was an extremely talented team with a number of

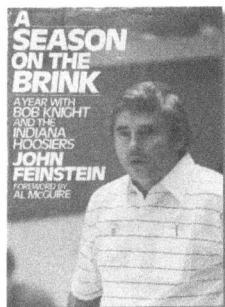

John Feinstein's best-seller took readers behind the scenes of Indiana University basketball.

human interest stories off the court as well. It was the final year of three Anderson high schools (consolidation to two schools would take place the following year) as well as the single class basketball tournament in Indiana, placing extra emphasis on this season.

While Feinstein took a leave of absence from *The Washington Post*, Phil and I were committed to taking on this project on top of our regular roles. Why wasn't this in the sports department? That three-man team simply had too much work already on a day-to-day basis (especially on game nights) to devote to an in-depth effort like this.

On the Sidelines

Let's start off the court with the angle of which Hollywood movies are made. Coach Ron Hecklinski was entering his fourth year at Anderson with a rather pedestrian 45-27 record. He had recorded just one losing season, though, in now 10 years as a head coach. He also spent one season as an assistant at Illinois State University and came to Anderson after four years on the bench at Ball State (the first of those as an assistant on the 1989-90 Sweet 16 team that lost to eventual champion UNLV).

In 1988, Hecklinksi had been diagnosed with Primary Sclerosing Cholangitis (PSC), a disease that attacks the bile ducts of the liver. There was no known cause – and no cure. Then 32 years old, he expected to need a liver transplant at some point in his life. Symptoms of the disease, including tiring more easily and weight loss, began to show up during his tenure at Ball State.

In May 1996, Hecklinksi was undergoing testing to check for the possibility of cancer (which would negate a transplant) when one of his veins burst. His doctor said in Phil's *Chasing the Dream: One Team's Quest for a State Championship* story (the title of our special season-long effort):

"We were looking for varices to see what his risk was and his risk was 100 percent. We were trying to stay out of the quicksand, and, in fact, we were standing in it."

On August 29 of that year, the call came that a liver was available. Th nearly 12-hour surgery took place the next day at the University of Kentucky Medical Center in Lexington. Although allowed to move into a nearby apartment a few weeks later, Hecklinksi did not return home to Anderson until nearly two months later – on October 28.

While the primary goal was going back to being a father to his 8-year-old daughter, he was also determined to return to teaching and coaching his team. He was courtside on day one, with most of his time spent sitting in a chair with a bullhorn by his side. The firsthand instruction would increase as he grew physically stronger during the season.

Months later, Hecklinski talked to Phil about the impacts of the life-saving surgery.

"I used to think my players used to miss shots on purpose just to piss me off. Or not guard anybody on purpose. I don't think that's really the case now. I see things in a more positive light.

"This time now, after the season, has been kind of special for me. Believe me there's been no mourning or period of time when I've said, 'Oh God, we lost.'

"That's different from every year of my life, because every time I've lost the last game as a player (an all-conference performer for two years at Manchester College in Wabash County) or coach it's been like the end of the world. But, because of what I've been through, my life's a little different now. It isn't the end of the world."

"The sun does come up," he concluded.

Guarding and Scoring

The players were a most interesting collection of teenagers with various backgrounds and back stories.

Tyson Jones and Eric Bush were a pair of ball-hawking guards, both under 6-feet tall, who also put up strong numbers on the offensive end of the court (14.8 points and 4.8 assists for Bush; 11.8 points and more than three assists for Jones). As the final two players introduced before every home game, they would always hear the message from Hecklinksi that "there's nobody better when you play together."

That didn't come naturally, however.

Jones' father, John Teague, played basketball at Anderson in the late 1950s. Half brothers John and Shawn were Indian stars, earning Division I scholarships to Boston University and Missouri, respectively. Jones was raised by his mother and listed her as his role model in life.

Bush's mother died in 1991 after several years of illness. His father spent time in prison and Bush lived with grandparents on both sides of the family before settling down with guardians Gary and Cindy Weatherford.

Jones was a standout shortstop on the baseball team and strong doubles player in tennis. He also used his voice talents in performances with the AHS Singers

Unlimited and AHS Madrigals.

Of all her son's activities, Beverly Jones only missed three innings of one baseball game. She had a good reason as she was matron of honor in a wedding. And she did skip the reception to get to the game.

Conversely, in the words of Bush, *"My whole year revolves around basketball. October through March we're in school. April through July is AAU. August is camps, September is conditioning."*

The difficult family circumstances caused him to admit, *"There was a time I really stopped caring."*

At one point in middle school, Bush was assigned to Cindy Weatherford's detention class. A relationship between the Weatherfords and Bush developed to the point where Cindy said with a smile, *"We were spending a lot of money on him, so we decided we should spend 24 hours a day with him."*

Bush's father was able to stay in his son's life and the solidified family situation helped lift Bush's work in school, where he carried a 3.2 grade point average.

Team Leader

On a team dominated by juniors, senior forward Aaron Boyd was the inspirational leader. His primary focuses were defense and rebounding – both coach and player said he possessed average basketball skills – but several offensive explosions came at the most opportune times.

Boyd was elevated to the varsity as a freshman under the most unusual circumstances. At school with the freshmen team only because of a mix-up in a tourney date, Boyd was summoned by Hecklinksi to go into the Saturday morning practice with the varsity. The coach liked what he saw and told him to return for the game that night.

In Boyd's words, *"I got there and coach said he was sitting in his office earlier and thinking, 'If I'm going to call this guy up, I might as well play him. If I'm going to play him, I might as well start him.' Shivers went through my body. I was really sweating."*

Four years later, Hecklinksi told his team in a postseason address: *"The program is where it's at because of Aaron Boyd. AB has helped erase this negative stigma that Anderson basketball had. It had a stigma attached to it that guys didn't go to class, guys are bad guys.*

"Aaron Boyd personally erased that stigma. ... Anytime I talk about the good of this program and what it does, Aaron Boyd's name will always be with that because

that's what you mean to me, Aaron, and that's what you mean to this program."

As Boyd departed for the final time, he shared with those remaining: *"You'd better cherish that locker room because it's hard leaving it."*

Unique Circumstance

In today's basketball game, nearly every team boasts one (or more) three-point shooting threats that can provide instant offense off the bench. Junior Jeremy Ramsey (7.5 points a game) filled that role for the Indians, shooting a team-best 37 percent from long range.

The 6-foot-6 "Rambo," as he was known to teammates, did not make the team at Madison Heights High School his freshman year. He dropped out of a school for a short time but re-emerged at Anderson and played mostly on the junior varsity as a sophomore.

Ramsey possessed the most unique situation off the court. In the locker room after the team's November 29 home opener, Hecklinksi announced a 4 p.m. practice the next day. Ramsey objected as he would be in church preparing to marry girlfriend Melissa Buckner. The couple was expecting a child the following summer.

The coach, aware of the wedding, was having a little fun. He added later that he certainly had not coached a married player during his high school career.

Melissa admits, *"I wasn't really a big basketball fan until I met him."* And while she said she was still learning the intricacies of the game, *"I tell Jeremy everything he did wrong (after games). I tell him he did a good job, but the first thing I point out is what he needs to work on – like defense."*

Missing in Action

While the 1996-97 Anderson Indians were among the most skilled teams in the state, perhaps the most talented player never took off his warmups in 21 of 26 games. Derrick Jones had earned a spot on the varsity as a freshman the year before as the team went 20-7 and lost in the semistate finals to eventual state champion Ben Davis. His fourth-quarter slam-dunk rebound in the sectional final ignited a rally from a double-digit deficit as he finished with 18 points and nine rebounds.

Jones played the first three games of his sophomore year before grades came out and he was declared academically ineligible. He would return for the final two games of the season but only after a series of negative incidents with coaches and fans.

Hecklinski had several chances to dismiss Jones from the team. He knew both the potential of the player and the risk of being cast aside.

"He would have been a very, very integral part of this team. We were a really good team. He would have been a guy that sent this team over the edge."

Despite attitude issues and comments to others that he didn't care anymore, Hecklinkski and freshman coach Brad Warner insisted Jones was hurting inside and covering up his true feelings.

Hecklinksi says, *"I didn't want Derrick to stray. I didn't want him to go and hang on the streets. Sometimes it's easy for kids when they're not involved. ... If we didn't stay with him, I thought we might have lost him a little bit."*

Jones returned for the final two games of the season but showed more rust than potential. What might have been remained an unknown. What was going to be was left for the next season.

Game Time

The question that remains is how this team performed on the court. The short answer: Good but not well enough.

Six days before Hecklinski's October return, assistant coach Terry Turner had warned that state and potentially even national recognition would lead to a "great big bullseye on your back from day one."

Game one was a matchup against perennial power Indianapolis North Central. Coaches had emphasized rebounding, stopping dribble penetration and defensive transition. Those were all drawbacks in an 82-78 opening loss for the third-ranked Indians.

The postgame message from Hecklinski was one that would be repeated several times during the season. *"Good teams are made in practice, on the practice floor. I can't tell you I'm glad this happened, but I can tell you I saw it coming."*

Eight straight wins followed, including a 76-67 North Central Conference win at Marion. It was the first Anderson road victory in the series in 18 years. The last of those eight wins came on December 28 – two months to the day that Hecklinski had returned home after his surgery.

The scene was New Castle (home of the world's largest high school gym) and the setting was the annual Hall of Fame Classic. The field included unbeaten teams DeKalb (ranked No. 5) and Batesville (No. 9) along with No. 6 Anderson and No. 17 Madison-Grant.

DeKalb featured Luke Recker, headed to Indiana University the following year and the early favorite for Mr. Basketball with a 32-point average. His team was leading 52-43 early in the fourth quarter. Hecklinski told his own players, with Recker within hearing distance, that Recker had shot DeKalb into the game and he'll shoot them out of it.

Recker takes some ill-advised shots with his team in the lead, then misses a pair of three-pointers in the final seconds as Anderson holds on for a 59-56 victory.

The second game of the day (Hecklinski went home and rested between contests but admitted he was tired for the nightcap) would come against Batesville, a small community along Interstate 74 in the southeastern part of the state (and only 15 miles from where I grew up). Batesville was the top rival of my school, East Central, and I had witnessed the Bulldogs dash dreams on a number of occasions. This Batesville team was fundamentally sound with an all-state guard in Michael Menser (my mother and his were close friends from working together in an elementary school).

Batesville dominated early but only led by two, 53-51, when Bush stole the ball and appeared to be on a breakaway before being dragged down at midcourt with 1:12 left. The official made the foul call but bypassed the intentional ruling that would have given Anderson two free throws and the ball. Hecklinksi makes his argument to no avail, heads back toward the bench and is suddenly whistled for a technical. Batesville gets two free throws and the ball, scores four points and pulls away for a 62-54 win.

Hecklinksi said he told the official, *"You know I had a liver transplant. I just jumped up as high as a I could on this call and my stomach is really sore where they cut me and it's all your fault."*

The Indians won nine straight to open the 1997 portion of the schedule. Many were closer than anticipated, with coaches bemoaning the gambling tendencies on defense that often backfired. Nevertheless, by mid-February the team moves up to No.1 in the state (with a 17-2 record).

There was a tourney atmosphere in the Wigwam on Valentine's Day with the top-ranked Indians hosting No. 4 New Castle. Foul trouble and errant three-point shooting were too much to overcome in a 67-61 defeat that cost the team an undisputed NCC title.

The team closed the regular season with two wins. But coaches and players were not pleased with the on-court performance, leading to two closed-door meetings in five days.

Tourney time was here. Sloppy first-half performances at home against Highland

and Frankton were overcome and the team earned a sectional title and improved its record to 21-3.

The advantage at the time of having a nearly 9,000-seat home gym is that you got to also host the regional round of the tournament. Anderson's last home regional loss was 20 years earlier. But like the Hall of Fame tourney in December, it was two games in one day. Anderson, now ranked fifth, takes on No. 6 Muncie South and played one of its better overall games to lead by 13 at the half in a 77-66 victory.

As the players settled down in front of their lockers (six hours before the title game), Hecklinski told them, *"This first game was on me. It was whether I could get this team ready to play a very, very good team. I had all week to do it. Now, the problem is, the next game is on you."*

Delta was the opponent. Located in adjoining Delaware County, northeast of Muncie, Delta did not play the same caliber of competition as the Indians. But after a 27-point loss to Muncie South early in the season, it won 17 of 19 games. And in a forewarning of what was to come, the best description of the regional final opponent is that it was a smart, fundamentally sound team capable of causing problems with its press and one which also excelled in a half-court game on both ends of the court.

In a nearly identical message to one he delivered before the Batesville game, Hecklinski said, *"This is their year. This is their state championship. Are you kidding me? A chance to play the Indians at the Wigwam? This is their state championship."*

Anderson had eight first-half turnovers. Its only second-period points were four free throws. Delta scored seven quick points to open the fourth period and was in control the rest of the way in a 56-48 triumph.

It wasn't David beating Goliath – or Milan beating Muncie Central in the 1954 state title game that inspired the movie *Hoosiers*. It was discipline and fundamentals winning out over individual talent. Delta won on to win the semistate and finish as state runner-up to Bloomington North, a team Anderson had defeated in overtime in the regular season.

Anderson finished with 22 wins in 26 games. While Hecklinski thanked the players on a personal level for being there for him in his recovery, he was also clear about what needed to improve (discipline, execution and a commitment to the weight room among the items) to allow for a more pleasing end to the following season.

It was a privilege and an honor to help capture this season in print. Hecklinski, his coaches, the players and their families were all most cooperative. It was my final sports "assignment" but not the last time I would have the opportunity to pair my writing with the world of sports.

CHASING the
DREAM
One Team's Quest for a State Championship

Bush-Jones a diverse backcourt duo

Following the Anderson High School
basketball team during the
1996-97 season resulted in
a compilation of stories
from both on and off the court.

Business of Sports

My next career journey took me to Indianapolis and the Indiana Chamber of Commerce. A statewide association for companies and their employees, the Indiana Chamber had a long history of success in legislative advocacy and providing business information.

As I arrived in April 1998, the Chamber was preparing to launch a new business magazine called *BizVoice*. Bimonthly issues (six a year) would highlight Indiana success stories and analyze topics important to the business community. In the words of the Chamber mission statement: "Cultivate a world-class environment which provides economic opportunity and prosperity for the people of Indiana and their enterprises."

BizVoice became the signature communication piece for the Chamber. It earned 100 state and national awards for writing and design excellence over an approximate two-decade period. Business and government leaders were among the interview subjects and those profiled in each issue.

One of the first articles that indirectly involved sports was an interview with Bill Cook, the 1999 Indiana Chamber Business Leader of the Year. Cook Group, which became a major medical device company, had its origins with Cook and his wife Gayle building stents in the spare bedroom of their home.

Despite 15 years of newspaper and other interviewing experience, I was one nervous guy heading to the office of the Bloomington entrepreneur and community stalwart. Cook was not especially fond of doing interviews. He was a little reluctant this time too but agreed with the coaxing of longtime friend and business partner

Steve Ferguson – a true Indiana Chamber champion for many years.

In doing my homework before the interview, I learned about two of Cook's passions: drum and bugle corps championships (on the edge of the sports spectrum) and professional basketball (he owned a team in Manchester, England). While at Ball State, I just happened to have a friend who was a drum and bugle corps competitor. And my wife was born in England and still had family living in Manchester.

Before getting down to the business of discussing business, I decided to break the ice by focusing on these two subjects. We spent about 25 minutes talking about Cook driving the bus for the Star of Indiana drum and bugle group that he founded and how he came to own the English basketball team (where he had important business connections).

I know the casual conversation relaxed me, and I think it did the same for Cook. He went on to share a multitude of business insights, including those below.

Asked what it takes to build a business or restore a historic structure (he was a leader in preserving old buildings – perhaps most famously the West Baden Springs hotel in French Lick, which was once dubbed the "Eighth Wonder of the World", spending millions of his own money), he said:

"It's a matter of risk taking and being prepared to make decisions and make them quickly. Our approach to business over the years has been that we believe in trying almost everything if it involves medicine. We found out you can't second guess whether any product is going to be essential."

As for the decision-making, Cook added, *"I found you can't do that with a committee; it has to be done personally. My personal belief is that many people use committees as a cop-out. I just never believed seeking a consensus was the best way to go. You have to have enough of an ego to believe you're right some of the time. I don't think I'm different than anyone else. I do like to take risks and the potential benefit that means."*

Another Annual Award winner, in 2006, was Indiana Governor Mitch Daniels. I did have the advantage of knowing him a little from his previous work at Eli Lilly and Company and some prior interviews.

The Daniels team gave us an opportunity to see the governor in action. We traveled to South Bend for a speech before riding in the RV he made famous during his first campaign (in 2004) to a discussion with law school students at Valparaiso University.

We asked as many questions, as well as shooting photos and video, as we could work into the trip. But we also needed to give the governor an opportunity to take care of some business and relax (a bit) before the next presentation. During that time, he sat in the front passenger seat of the RV, reading the *USA Today* sports section.

Knowing he was a Los Angeles Dodgers fan, I mentioned the four consecutive home runs the Dodgers had hit in a game earlier that week. We then engaged in a wide-ranging sports conversation, and I learned that Daniels (just like so many of us) strives to watch ESPN's SportsCenter to catch up on the highlights he might have missed.

Two years later, Daniels' predecessor as governor – Joe Kernan – was honored for his work as co-chair of the Indiana Commission on Local Government Reform. He and Randall Shepard, chief justice of the Indiana Supreme Court, led an important effort to modernize an outdated local government system. The bottom line was to serve taxpayers more efficiently and effectively.

Kernan was a Navy pilot when his plane was shot down in Vietnam in February 1972. He was detained as a prisoner of war for nearly 11 months. Later, he was a popular three-term mayor of South Bend before serving as lieutenant governor. He became governor when Frank O'Bannon died in office in 2003.

But Kernan's past and present, at the time, revolved around baseball. He was an infielder, and later a catcher, at Notre Dame. After being defeated by Daniels in the 2004 gubernatorial election, he returned home to South Bend for another diamond mission as president and managing investor of the South Bend Silver Hawks Class A team.

"I got involved because I feared new ownership, in all probability, would be from outside the community and move the franchise from South Bend," Kernan related. "The deal closed on September 15, 2006, and since that time I've been busier than anticipated. But I love being around baseball, and we've put together a great team and front office."

Both my interview with Kernan and our video shoot took place at Coveleski Stadium (Stanley Coveleski was a Hall of Famer who settled in South Bend after his playing career ended). After all, it was Kernan's "office". We sat in the stands while batting practice was going on, mixing local government conversation with recollections from his days as a player and longtime fan.

The overall goal for Kernan and the city was to bring people into downtown for an entertainment option and to help stimulate private investment. It was also a little more basic for Kernan – *"for me, it's making sure kids and families that might not have the chance to come to a ballgame get the opportunity to come here."*

The Silver Hawks and Notre Dame played a first-ever exhibition game in the spring of 2008. Owner Jeff Moorad of the Arizona Diamondbacks (the parent club of the South Bend team) called Kernan the day before the game and said he wanted to sign the 62-year-old to a one-day contract so he could participate.

"I ended up playing a couple of innings at second base. I struck out, but I went down swinging," stated Kernan, who occasionally during the season "shagged fly balls" with the team during batting practice.

The Annual Award winners were honored each year at a business celebration that featured a nationally known keynote speaker. Sports played a prominent role here also.

Bob Costas did the honors in 2005. Our interview previewing the event touched on many of his career highlights – Olympic hosting, baseball play-by-play, Triple Crown horse racing, boxing and so much more.

Costas hosted the opening of Conseco Fieldhouse (home of the Indiana Pacers) in November 1999 when Indiana honored its 50 greatest basketball players of all time. The night was memorable – "I can't imagine a similar ceremony opening the Alamodome," he deadpans – but says it's the facility that offers the ongoing tribute.

"It's the best arena in the NBA. They took the lead of Camden Yards (Baltimore) in baseball. It's a modern facility with its fan content, amenities and revenue-generating capabilities, but it pays tribute to the history of the game. It has a connection to generations of history. It's important that it's called a fieldhouse. It's a perfect fit for the city, the state and the team."

Costas entertained the audience with stories from throughout his broadcasting career.

A household name in news broadcasting, Tom Brokaw, fell into the Bill Cook mold. My time for a phone conversation with the NBC news host was limited. The interview was not going particularly well – Brokaw seemed distracted and who could blame him as I'm sure there were more pressing issues in his life than talking to some magazine editor in Indiana – so I pulled out the sports card in mentioning John Wooden.

Wooden had passed away a few days earlier. I had read that while working for NBC in Los Angeles early in his career, Brokaw became a big fan of UCLA and the legendary coach who got his start as a player and coach in Indiana.

We talked about Wooden for a while and the remainder of the interview went smoothly.

Brokaw was asked about people who left a lasting impression on him beyond the story:

"Well, you know Coach Wooden was right at the top of those ranks. I lived in Los Angeles when he had his great run. I was there from 1966 to 1973, and my closest friends were UCLA graduates. I was thinking about this the other day. The cherished moment was when they secured their season tickets every year. And I was able to go to the games, and I got to know him a little bit. And the last few years whenever there would be a birthday celebration, I would be asked to record a greeting to him or to send something, because he also was a member of the Greatest Generation.

"Bill Walton was on (TV) this morning, and I remember when Bill came to UCLA, he was really a hippie. And he was a social activist. And Coach Wooden said, 'You gotta get your hair cut, Bill, or you're off the team.' And they had some real differences. And Bill told me a few years ago, he said, 'You know, I just didn't believe in all that stuff when I arrived there. But when I started raising my own children, I found that I was printing out Coach Wooden's sayings and putting them in their lunch boxes so that they would have the same exposure to wisdom that I did.'"

Terry Bradshaw, the four-time Super Bowl winning quarterback for the Pittsburgh Steelers and Fox broadcaster, was the Annual Dinner speaker in 2011. That happened to be the year Colts quarterback Peyton Manning was out for the season after a series of neck surgeries. Kerry Collins and Curtis Painter were the primary fill-ins and the team lost its first 13 games in compiling a 2-14 record.

The Chamber's conference and events team always did an excellent job of taking care of the keynote speakers – from meeting them at the airport and securing everything needed prior to the event that evening. Bradshaw was one of the few to pass on any assistance, giving assurances that he would be at the right place at the right time.

He made it – barely – for a pre-dinner media obligation. In his rambling, folksy style, he said all the right things when questioned about the then 0-8 Colts, the Super Bowl that was coming to Indianapolis at the end of that season and other topics of the day.

As soon as the interview with local reporters ended, he turned to myself and a Chamber colleague and drawled something to the effect of, "I knew the Colts would struggle without Manning, but I never thought they would be this damn bad."

By the way, Bradshaw put on an excellent show. He embraced the post-football persona he had developed over many years, making fun of himself first and foremost. In the post-event meet-and-greet, local Steeler fans brought their Terrible Towels and souvenir footballs. I will have more on the rival of the Cincinnati Bengals later.

Sports played into interviews with
and presentations from Indiana Chamber
Annual Dinner speakers Bob Costas (top left),
Tom Brokaw (top right) and Terry Bradshaw.

Indiana governors Joe Kernan (bottom left)
and Mitch Daniels were also big baseball fans.

CHAPTER 8

Telling the Stories

In the bimonthly *BizVoice*, a popular strategy was to publish a series of related stories throughout a calendar year. In 2014, one of the focuses was on the Business of Sports. Among the highlights:

- Profiling Jonathan Bender, who was making the transformation from an NBA career plagued by injuries to becoming an entrepreneur.

A No. 5 choice in the 1999 draft, Bender never fully realized his potential on the court. His slender 7-foot frame led to a series of medical issues. Following retirement, he created a device to help users build leg strength without stressing their knees.

Bender talked about attributes shared by athletes and entrepreneurs: *"Determination, consistency and being able to stay focused on one thing even if you've failed in some areas over and over – and the work ethic."*

- Digonex was an Indianapolis-based business at the forefront of dynamic pricing – adjusting ticket prices for sporting events based on the quality or attractiveness of the opposition. In the baseball world, that means higher costs, for example, when the popular Chicago Cubs are in town compared to the Pittsburgh Pirates.

The strategy is widely popular today but was in its infancy at that time. Digonex developed its own mechanism – the Sports and Entertainment Analytical Ticketing System (SEATS). It used complex algorithms to help teams earn maximum revenue by adjusting prices.

Digonex CEO Jan Eglen on the growing dynamic pricing trend in sports ticketing: *"You don't always have to increase prices in order to increase revenues. You need to price smarter. Sometimes, you can drop prices to get more people in the seats, and make more money on the ancillaries like merchandise, food and parking."*

• Professional soccer came to Indiana with the formation of the Indy Eleven. The team began play in the North American Soccer League, a tier below Major League Soccer.

While there were a number of close losses in the inaugural season, the team led the league in attendance by a wide margin and established itself in the community with a number of sponsorships and partnerships.

Ersal Ozdemir, a native of Turkey and owner of a local construction company, discussed his motivation: *"This is the wealthiest country in the world. We think we can have one of the best soccer leagues in the world. We can be competitive and as fan support grows, we can get better and afford to pay more for players and hope to get to the same level as European and South American soccer."*

• Part of the reason for compiling this series was Indianapolis' long-held status as the amateur sports capital of the world. It was a strategy that had been developed and executed on over more than 30 years.

Four Olympic national governing bodies – in track and field, gymnastics, diving and synchronized swimming – called Indianapolis home at that time. There was an ongoing economic and cultural impact due to the meetings, events and Indiana business partners that were part of the mix.

One of the leaders of those governing bodies noted: *"What makes a city special is when you feel like you own the town. You can showcase sports here because you can own it. That's not always the case in bigger cities."*

A sidebar told the story of the Indiana University Natatorium, one of the top swimming and diving venues in the country. Those who qualify for the Olympics have their names painted on the back wall as a legacy of their accomplishments and an inspiration for the next generation.

I talked with David Boudia, who grew up in Noblesville and earned Olympics gold in 2012 in London in platform diving. The downtown Indianapolis facility became as close as one can get to a second home.

"Six days a week for seven straight years at the Natatorium," Boudia reflected.

"2008 was probably the biggest home field advantage when the Olympic Trials were in Indianapolis. That was one of the most special competitions I had ever been in because it was local, because of family and friends being able to come. And it was the iconic names of the Olympians on the back wall of the Natatorium. Every day

growing up I went to practice and saw those names on the wall, and that's part of the package of becoming an Olympian."

- We examined the impact of cycling and biking through the eyes of a community, university, company and business leader.

Bloomington, Indiana had earned a silver-accredited "Bicycle Friendly Community" recognition from the League of American Bicyclists. Its B-Line Trail – a 3.1-mile multi-use trail that cuts through downtown – had benefited the area in many ways. Marian University's cycling team boasted 26 national championships since 1992. The Knights were among the nation's leading cycling programs.

Indianapolis' west side is home to one of the world's most notable cycling companies: Zipp Speed Weaponry (and its parent company, Chicago-based SRAM) boasted high-profile clients such as 2008 Tour de France winner Carlos Sastre (of Spain). Bill Browne, founding principal/president of RATIO Architects, Inc. in Indianapolis, mixed business with pleasure to enrich Central Indiana's biking community. Browne was instrumental in designing PowerBooster (Marian University's indoor cycling training business, which helped fund the team).

- Female tennis and golf professionals were relying on an Indiana university and company to enhance their lives off the court and course.

Tennis star Venus Williams enrolled at Indiana University (IU) East to pursue her bachelor's degree in 2011. That led to a partnership between the Women's Tennis Association (WTA) and the school. As of fall 2013, IU East was the exclusive partner of the WTA for online bachelor's degrees for women's professional tennis players.

Williams: *"There has to be life after the sport. As an athlete, you end so early … and you have to figure out who you are and what you do. I'm excited that these other players are figuring that out."*

Since 2009, Indianapolis-based Language Training Center (LTC) has had an agreement with the Ladies Professional Golf Association to offer language and cultural training. It's also served a variety of other professional athletic groups.

Iconic Venues

Another *BizVoice* series was titled Road Trip Treasures, taking readers to various parts of the state for both popular destinations and little-known attractions.

For basketball aficionados, Indiana has no shortage of historic locations that offer vivid reminders of Hoosiers' passion for the sport. Three of the most special destinations can be enjoyed within 15 miles of each other in Henry County (40 miles east of Indianapolis).

Hoosier Gym in Knightstown is most famous as the home of the Hickory Huskers in the 1986 movie *Hoosiers*. More than 65,000 people were expected to visit in 2017 to enjoy the nostalgia as well as the more than 80 high school basketball games scheduled for the facility in the 2017-2018 season.

The Indiana Basketball Hall of Fame had welcomed more than 300,000 guests from around the country and globe since relocating to New Castle in 1990. Chris May, executive director for the last eight and half years, appropriately referred to his job as "walking into arguably one of the holiest of holy places in Indiana."

A short walk from the Hall of Fame takes you to New Castle High School Fieldhouse, with the banner inside proudly proclaiming it as the "the largest and finest high school fieldhouse in the world." Its 9,300-plus seats exceeded the capacity of, among others, the basketball homes of both Duke and Notre Dame universities.

Bob Garner said he was a benchwarmer on the last Knightstown High School team (1966) to use the Hoosier Gym as its home court. The facility had been built for $14,000 in 1921. Garner returned home to be the events coordinator for the historic venue.

"Parents and coaches want their teams to come and play here because they love the movie; the impact on the kids after they are here is equal to the parents," Garner reported.

Need proof. On December 22, 2017, two Mississippi rivals and their fans traveled to Knightstown to play four games. It all started with a dad and his son visiting Hoosier Gym the previous summer. *"The son says, 'Dad, I've got to play a game here,'* Garner recalls. *"The dad, who was his coach, says, 'I don't know how we can pull that off.'*

"He calls me up a few days later and says one of our rivals wants to come here and play," Garner continued. *"About three days later, he asks if they could play two games that day. My parents said, 'If the varsity is coming, the JV is coming.' Not a week goes by before I get a call from the athletic director, asking, 'Can we play two more games (varsity and JV girls)?'*

That's how East Webster and Pontotoc – and many fans – came approximately 700 miles from Mississippi to Indiana three days before Christmas. Area hotels, restaurants and businesses were among the beneficiaries. A team from Syracuse, New York, played in the Hoosier Gym. An Illinois athletic director told Garner he "would like to play here every year if he could." Two Ohio schools were set for the coming season, and the Ohio High School Athletic Association wanted to bring 12 teams in the following year for a six-game extravaganza.

The Hoosier Gym had long been a shrine to the film that tops more than a few "best sports movie of all time" lists. Photos and other memorabilia greet visitors upon their arrival.

But they come to see the locker room. And the bench where Gene Hackman (playing *Hoosiers* coach Norman Dale) sat while famously proclaiming "my team is on the floor" in refusing to put a player he disciplined back into the game. As well as where town drunk Wilber "Shooter" Flatch (played by Dennis Hopper and father of one of the team's players) was positioned in the stands during various scenes.

Back to Garner and just a few of his experiences. *"A young man from Oregon comes in, walks in the door and starts crying. I didn't know how to react. This place has this effect on a lot of people. He says, 'I played high school basketball and my dad was the town drunk.' I almost started crying."* Or there's the woman who informed her husband of his pending fatherhood by holding up a Hickory onesie she purchased at the gift shop. *"What a way to find out,"* Garner adds with a smile. *"He (the dad to be) starts crying. That was a great one."*

A popular pregame video produced by the Indiana Pacers contains the line: "In 49 states, it's just basketball. But this … IS INDIANA!" Never were truer words spoken.

The Indiana University Natatorium remains the "holy grail" for Olympic diving hopefuls.

Businessman Ersal Ozdemir brought professional soccer to Indiana.

Visitors can see the famed home basketball court from the movie *Hoosiers*.

CHAPTER 9

One of the Boys of Summer

The final in-depth *BizVoice* magazine series I worked on was in 2019. Indiana Icons was the theme. As the title suggests, we were going to go in-depth on some of the Hoosiers who had the most significant contributions to the state over the years.

Two of those just happened to be legendary sports figures. Having the opportunity to tell their stories was a true privilege.

Carl Erskine was about to turn 92 years old when I sat down with him in late 2018 at the retirement community where he lived in his hometown of Anderson (yes, it was back to the city where I had worked 30 years prior). The three hours I spent with Erskine clearly rank near the top on my list of all-time favorite interviews.

Here is the beginning of my *BizVoice* story, headlined "King of the Hill: Erskine Stands Tall in Game, Hometown":

In 1953, Anderson native Carl Erskine won 20 games (losing six) for the Brooklyn Dodgers. He was going to get three starts, if necessary, in the World Series against the nemesis New York Yankees. After a rare poor performance in the opener, Erskine came back two days later in Game 3 (no travel time required). The result was a then-World Series record 14 strikeouts, including four K's against Yankee legend Mickey Mantle. It was October 2, 1953.

In recounting the story of that game, Erskine rattled off the names of the pinch-hitters he faced in the ninth inning, how many pitches – and what they were – required to record the final two strikeouts and his nervousness in facing the final batter of the game, knowing that one swing of the bat could turn victory into defeat.

In the day between those two games, Erskine recalls, "*I told Duke (Snider, his roommate), 'I've got to pitch like there is no tomorrow. I was counted on for three starts in this series. I already blew one and we're behind two games.'*"

Sixty-five years later, sitting in a quiet area of the retirement community where he and his wife, Betty, now live, Erskine recounts the lesson from that day. "*I tell kids: Don't ever get bothered by failure. If you handle it right, it's the greatest motivator you will ever have not to do it again. When you're given a responsibility and you don't come up to it,*" he continues, "*you've got to deal with it in a way that says, 'I can't let that happen again.' That failure, I think, was the biggest motivator in my baseball days. Down deep in my gut, I just bitterly hated how I pitched that opening game and disappointed (manager Chuck) Dressen.*"

Erskine won 122 games between 1948 and 1959. He appeared in 11 games in five different World Series (earning two rings) and pitched two no-hitters for the team known as the *Boys of Summer* (as chronicled by author Roger Kahn). Shoulder problems helped end his career in 1959 at the age of 32.

It was off the field that Erskine earned his icon status. He returned home to become a business and community leader.

Carl and Betty Erskine's fourth child, son Jimmy, was born in 1960 with Down syndrome, then known as mongolism. It was an "ugly" term, with a dim future for those inflicted with the disease. Years later Eunice Kennedy Shriver, founder of the Special Olympics, asked Erskine to come to the nation's capital to make a presentation on behalf of the program. Before leaving home, he grabbed two items.

At the Kennedy Center in Washington, he made this greatest "pitch" of all. He recalled the words.

"*I wore my World Series ring today because this is a major event, so I got it out of my lockbox. I remember when I got this ring. We were like little boys; we couldn't stand still. We were all so excited. What could be more achievable than owning a World Series ring!*" Then Erskine reached in the pocket of his blazer and pulled out a gold medal.

"*Let me show you something else,*" he shared with the audience. "*This is my son Jimmy's championship medal in the state games in Terre Haute, Indiana, in the 50-meter freestyle. Now, this ring represents Hall of Famers, superstars, gifted athletes – we're supposed to win. But was anybody ever expecting a special needs kid to be competitive and win a gold medal? So I ask you, 'Which is the greater achievement?'*" Shriver was so moved that she asked Erskine to appear at other events around the country to repeat his story. He did over the course of several years.

Jackie Robinson, who integrated the sport as the first black player, was already with the Dodgers when Erskine was in the minor league system in Fort Worth, Texas. The young pitcher faced Robinson in an exhibition game.

"(After the game) he came across the field, called my out by name and said, "Young man, I hit against you twice today. You're not going to be here very long." Erskine was called up to the big leagues a few months later and the two began a friendship that extended well beyond the baseball field. Racial differences meant nothing to Erskine. One of his best friends growing up was Jumpin' Johnny Wilson, the star on Anderson's 1946 state championship basketball team.

He was an eyewitness to history, noting Robinson's "biggest skill was self-control. You can't imagine what he went through and never fought back." With his son Jimmy, Erskine and his family were active participants in another form of evolutionary progress. He wrote about the two in a book titled *The Parallel*.

"My nine seasons as a teammate and friend of Jackie Robinson gave me a close-up experience watching this super talented black athlete beat segregation. And then in the same lifetime experience a parallel journey with my son, Jimmy, born with Down's syndrome who would face prejudice, exclusion and rejection similar in many ways to Jackie's."

In our conversation, he added, *"There's dignity involved where dignity didn't exist. What really mattered in my career was the cultural change that Jackie caused and the population change in what my son Jimmy benefited from."*

The Erskine story concluded with these thoughts:

Despite a 5-foot-10½, 165-pound frame, Erskine was a hard thrower with good movement on his fastball and a sharp-breaking overhand curve. He reflected on beating rival Muncie Central in high school and being stopped after the game by Delaware County legend Odie Barnett, who told him: "Son, let me tell you something. Don't ever let anybody tell you you're too small."

During his career in Brooklyn, he was always proudly referred to by a writer from The New York Times as "the gentleman from Indiana." Asked now about the greatest honor he has ever received or what he is most proud of, it's not too difficult to determine his answer in advance.

"When you sort them all out, marrying my wife Betty ... we just celebrated our 71st anniversary. We have four children. The headlines, the trophies, the rings all pale in comparison to having a mate for life, a family. I know that's a standard answer. Personally, Betty and I have had a good strong faith life. I think that's basic to a full life. The personal achievements ... they get to be less and less important.

"I never dreamed ever of winning a World Series ring. But when it happened, I was proud of it. But what does that mean. Not too much. Playing in the majors is a rare experience. I got to do that with a great historic team. A skinny kid from the west side of Anderson; it's been such an unbelievable ride for me. I've had good health for a long time, you can't beat that. I think when it's all said and done, I'd settle on family."

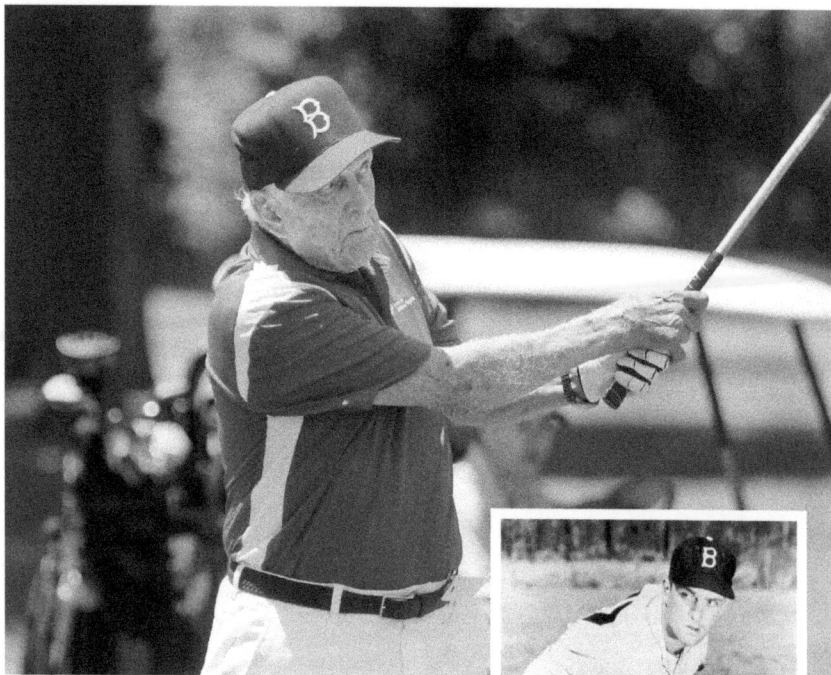

Carl Erskine, whether pitching on the mound in his playing days or hitting the links at a local golf course, is an even greater person than athlete.

CHAPTER 18

Golf's First Couple

Later in 2019, it took two issues and 18 "holes" to recount the careers of golf course architects Pete and Alice Dye.

Alice, an Indianapolis native, passed away early that year three weeks short of her 92nd birthday. She was commonly known as the "First Lady" of golf course architecture. Pete, age 93 and suffering from advanced Alzheimer's, was generally regarded as changing the game of golf with his unique style and attention to detail. Add in sons Perry and P.B., prolific golf course designers in their own rights, and you had America's "First Family of Golf."

The challenge for me was telling the story of Pete and Alice without having the opportunity to talk to either one. Fortunately, their sons were more than ready to discuss the family business and many others in the sport and beyond had their own anecdotes to share.

At the top of that list was golf legend Jack Nicklaus. In the category of 15-minute telephone interviews, which I have conducted thousands of times, this was a tough one to beat.

I had researched the Dye-Nicklaus connection, reached out through the Nicklaus Companies and received a positive response that "The Golden Bear" would be happy to talk. The timing, however, was still up in the air.

I was pleasantly surprised a few days later to be sitting at my desk when the phone rang with Columbus, Ohio listed on the caller ID and the person on the other end saying, "This is Jack Nicklaus. Is this Tom?"

The setup: As a high school junior, Pete won the individual title at the Ohio High School Golf Championship. In 1957, he qualified for the U.S. Open. Although he didn't make the cut, his score equaled that of Arnold Palmer and was eight shots better than the 17-year-old Nicklaus. Later that same year, a fundraising exhibition at an Urbana, Ohio course (designed by Pete's father in 1922) featured Nicklaus, Sam Snead (winner of a record 82 PGA Tour events), Pete and Bob Ross Jr., the reigning Ohio Amateur champ. Final scores on that day: Snead, 70; Dye, 71; Nicklaus, 75; and Ross, 76.

The design connection: When building The Golf Club in central Ohio in the mid-1960s, Pete brought Nicklaus to the site to get his insight on a few of the hole designs. In 1969, Nicklaus was asked by real estate developer Charles Fraser to assist with creating what became the Harbour Town course at Hilton Head in South Carolina. When Nicklaus said he didn't know how to design a golf course but was aware of someone who did, Fraser responded that he had never heard of Pete. Nicklaus' reply: "You will."

Nicklaus lays out the partnership. *"The fee was $40,000. I made 23 visits there in a Lear jet. We got done with the golf course and Pete had taken the $40,000 we made and put it back in the golf course and I never got reimbursed a dime for my airplane.*

"I said, 'That's not a very good business deal.' He said, 'That's what we do.'"

The partnership extended to several more courses, with Alice also involved. *"I said, 'Pete, I love the experience, but I can't afford you.' He put our design fee back into every golf course. It was a great learning experience, and I had a blast doing it."*

Nicklaus, the winner of a record 18 major tournaments, went on to design more than 400 courses in 45 countries. *"If Pete had never called me, I never would have gone out there, never would have got involved at Harbour Town and never would have had this career. I just think Pete was way ahead of his time. He did things that nobody else would do. He took a chance on them and that's why he was so good. He was just brilliant at what he did."*

In fact, the Dyes were brilliant together.

As a child, Alice Holliday O'Neal would ride her bicycle to play golf at Indianapolis' Woodstock Country Club. At age 15, she won the Indiana State Junior and Woodstock Club championships. Among her career accomplishments:

- 50 amateur championships, including nine for the state of Indiana and 11 in the Indianapolis city tournament.
- Two United States Senior Women's Amateur Championships and a pair of Canadian Senior tournaments.

- Played on the U.S. team in the 1970 Curtis Cup, the biennial amateur competition between the United States and Great Britain/Ireland.

Alice was the first female member of the American Society of Golf Course Architects and the first woman to serve as a director of the PGA of America. As evidence of their partnership, Pete was stymied in what to do with what became the famous 17th hole "Island Green" at the Tournament Players Club (TPC) Sawgrass in Florida.

When Alice suggested he put the green in the middle and fill up the big hole around it with water, Pete balked.

Friend Curt Miller picks up the story. *"Pete took out a seven iron, hit it in the middle of the green and said it's too easy.* Alice's response was, *'It's easy with me and the frog watching. Put 10,000 people out here and it won't be easy.'"*

The rest, as they say, is history.

Son P.B. ranked these courses as his parents' top designs: Harbour Town (1969); TPC Sawgrass-Stadium Course (1982) at Ponte Vedra Beach, just south of Jacksonville, Florida; The Ocean Course (1991) at Kiawah Island, South Carolina, built for the 1991 Ryder Cup that became known as "The War by the Shore"; The Golf Club (1967) in New Albany, Ohio, outside Columbus; Oak Tree Golf Club (1976) in Edmond, Oklahoma; and PGA West-Stadium Course (1986) in La Quinta, California.

"Dad was not a golf course architect," P.B. insisted. *"He literally goes on site and runs the job. He's a designer, a construction manager. We call ourselves ditch diggers. We figure it out as it goes, what work needs to be done at that moment.*

"He did everything he could to screw with the professional's eyes, to make his eyes lie to him. Be as deceptive visually as you can. He does everything he can to make you think. Because we all know in golf as soon as you start to think, you mess up."

In Indiana, any discussion of top courses starts with French Lick Resort.

Steve Ferguson, chairman of the Cook Group who set up my interview with Bill Cook, gave Pete an aerial photo and topographical drawings of the proposed course site. The reported response was, "I don't think I can build a golf course there." The two drove around and through as much of the wooded area as they could anyway. By the middle of the next week, Pete had sketched a course layout onto a napkin.

This was 2005. Construction began in April 2006 and The Pete Dye Course at French Lick opened in 2009. It has become a premier destination for golfers from around the country and beyond. *"The thing that separated Pete was that you could just tell it was going to be personal to him,"* Ferguson said. *"It wasn't just a business deal. What really persuaded me that he was the guy was his passion."*

Speaking of deals, Pete was not a big fan of the business side of his work. There are multiple accounts of meetings with lawyers and others prior to starting a new project. Pete's mantra, paraphrased: "I don't do contracts. He (the owner) can fire me anytime he wants to and if he's not happy, he doesn't have to pay me."

The response from the person(s) who wanted the Dye magic to happen: "When are you going to start?" There are more than a few examples of Pete charging a grand total of $1 for work on college courses. On the other hand, Miller (a 52-year member of Crooked Stick Golf Club in Carmel, Indiana where the Dyes got their start and which later became their home) said he was president when Pete was upgrading the course for the upcoming PGA tournament (1991). "I had to battle him because he's not real familiar with a budget."

Ferguson drew an insightful comparison between his longtime boss and close friend, Bill Cook, and Pete.

"Pete is a visual guy, like Bill Cook. He didn't give you a set of plans. About one in 2,000 people have an imagination; fewer than that have real vision," Ferguson contended. *"Bill Cook had real vision. He could look at something as it was and see how it could be. Pete was the same way about golf courses. He could look at a piece of ground and visualize how it was going to be."*

One more similarity, courtesy of Ferguson. *"Bill Cook, we put $35 million into West Baden Hotel on a handshake. Pete Dye built a course on a handshake. Pete was just one of those people with special visons and abilities. In a lot of respects, he changed the game of golf."*

Wayne Timberman, a close friend of the Dyes for 70 years: *"Pete was the artist with all the creativity and Alice the pragmatist. That was a good combination."* He adds that Pete *"was good on the stage. To my knowledge, he never prepared a speech. He's the only guy I know who literally did what he wanted to do every day of his life."*

Golf course designers Pete and Alice Dye in their early years and
remembered in bronze at Crooked Stick Golf Club
in Carmel, Indiana.

CHAPTER 11

Diamond Gems

opened this journey with a brief description of my hometown of St. Leon. Although located in Indiana, we were really much more closely aligned – economically and sports-wise – with Cincinnati, Ohio. On a professional level, that means deep allegiances to the baseball Reds and football Bengals.

How deep? The story I have told for many years is that St. Leon consisted of about 600 residents (true) and about 400 (maybe slightly exaggerated, maybe not) were related to me. Two of those relatives were my aunts who were Catholic nuns. They not only loved attending games in Cincinnati but were devoted viewers and listeners – the more popular option in those days.

When we were together for a wedding or other family event, I was often responsible for sneaking off to the car to listen to the radio and report back on the latest development in the Reds' game. Sister Paulita and Sister Inez were true fans and certainly influenced my love for the home team.

From 1912 to 1970, the Reds played at what became known as Crosley Field. It was among the smallest ballparks in the majors with a capacity of less than 30,000. I recall attending several games there and remember reading that the longest home run in history came there off the bat of slugging catcher Ernie Lombardi. His blast cleared a sign in left field that offered a free suit to anyone hitting it, landed in the back of a truck traveling on the nearby interstate and traveled a reported 30 miles.

The Reds moved to downtown's Riverfront Stadium in the middle of the 1970 season. Similar to Three Rivers in Pittsburgh and Busch Stadium in St. Louis, Riverfront was a circular design that was home to both professional baseball and football. The opener at Riverfront came at the end of June; two weeks later, in the All-Star Game, hometown hero Pete Rose bowled over Cleveland catcher Ray Fosse in the 12th inning to score the winning run. (Much more to come on Rose, my on-field hero as a youngster).

As an 8-year-old that season, I was perched in the first row of the centerfield stands for the opening game of the 1970 World Series. Not only did I watch Baltimore third baseman Brooks Robinson imitate a vacuum cleaner in corralling everything hit in his direction, but I was on hand for what remains one of the most controversial plays in World Series history.

The Reds' Bernie Carbo attempted to score from third on a chopper back to the mound. Carbo was tagged by the glove of catcher Elrod Hendricks, but both players slammed into umpire Ken Burkhart. The umpire failed to notice that Hendricks had the ball in his bare hand when he put the tag on Carbo with his glove. The out call stood – no multiple camera angles or replays at that time – and the Orioles went on to win the opener and the Series four games to one.

With family and friends, I witnessed a selection of games over the next few years as the Reds advanced to the World Series in 1972 (losing to Oakland) before winning back-to-back titles in 1975 (Red Sox) and 1976 (Yankees). The home team was known as the Big Red Machine for its star-studded lineup that featured Rose, Joe Morgan, Johnny Bench, Tony Perez and more.

Many of those games included my father, who listened to and watched Reds games religiously. He enjoyed the in-person viewing but was also practical as he needed to leave very early on weekday mornings for his job on a General Motors assembly line in Hamilton, Ohio. As the game neared the final inning, we would move to a standing position behind the seats closest to a nearby exit.

If the final out was a routine fly ball, for example, I would be waiting for that catch while Dad was rapidly making his way toward the gate. It was all I could do to catch up and not be left behind.

The fate of the Reds – often the struggles and not the triumphs – would be a constant topic of conversation whenever I visited my parents over the 30-plus years they were alive after I completed college. Dad always had an opinion on what could be done to improve the team's fortunes, and he was usually right.

Although 1978 was not a playoff season for the team, I was able to witness two special occasions within six weeks. In May of that year, Rose collected the 3,000th hit of his career. The pitcher was Montreal ace Steve Rogers and the Expos first baseman was longtime Rose teammate and close friend Perez.

In June of that year, on a Friday night against the St. Louis Cardinals, Tom Seaver recorded the only no-hitter of his career. The Reds had acquired Seaver a year earlier from the New York Mets (where he had two hitless games broken up in the ninth inning). He survived a couple of walks before retiring George Hendrick on a grounder to first baseman Dan Driessen for the final out.

Thorns in a Rose

I promised more on Pete Rose. He was Charley Hustle, unfortunately in more ways than one. As a player, there was nothing not to like. He ran to first base when receiving a base on balls (hence, the nickname which came from Yankees star Mickey Mantle in spring training). He would slide headfirst or, as he did in that 1970 All-Star Game, run over anyone who was in the way of his or his team's success.

Rose grew up in Cincinnati and epitomized the blue-collar nature of the city. He played where the team needed him, becoming the only person in major league history to start at least 50 games at five different positions: second base, right field, left field, third base and first base. In 1978, the 15th and final season of his first stint with the Reds, Rose captivated the country with a 44-game hitting streak (tying the National League record as the closest challenger to Joe DiMaggio and his record 56 games).

After the 1978 season, Philadelphia thought the 37-year-old Rose could be the difference for a successful team that had not been able to make the World Series. They made Rose the highest-paid athlete in team sports up to that point with $3.2 million over four years. Oh, how the times have changed.

Fast forward to 1984 and Rose returns to Cincinnati as player-manager. He breaks Ty Cobb's all-time hit record in May 1985 and finishes his playing career a year later with 4,192 hits. His success as a manager is mixed, but he returns to the spotlight – in a most negative way – in 1989 with the investigation into his gambling habits (including betting on baseball) and his ultimate suspension from the game.

Again, I was working as a sportswriter in Anderson at the time. My boss was an ardent Dodger fan, the Reds' biggest rival during much of Rose's career. We battled verbally, and sometimes in print, over the allegations, the evidence and the final decision. I, like many other fans, just couldn't believe that the person we admired so much as kids would break the most basic rule of the game.

Another Anderson newspaper colleague grew up in New York and was a big Mets fan. The two of us, and our wives, traveled to Cincinnati for a pair of games over the July 4 weekend as the Rose controversy was reaching its peak. CNN was on hand prior to the game to collect fan perspectives. With our respective Reds and Mets jerseys on display, we were corralled by the reporter.

Maybe I was a little biased, but I thought both of us made legitimate points as we answered questions and debated Rose's innocence or guilt. Apparently, we sounded a bit too good as the piece that aired that evening was slanted heavily in favor of sensationalistic comments that are often more appealing to the audience.

As it turned out, the same brashness and confidence in his abilities that allowed Rose to thrive on the field spearheaded his downfall. He claims he never bet against the Reds, which was also included in the Dowd Report that was used to justify the suspension. If that is accurate, I believe Rose thought he would simply capitalize on his managerial skills to help the team win more games – and himself some extra money.

Maybe that's still a naïve outlook. But you can't convince me that Rose does not belong in the Hall of Fame based on his achievements on the field. There is no shortage of "bad actors" enshrined in Cooperstown. Unfortunately, it appears the now 82-year-old Rose will never see the honor he so richly deserves.

One more Rose tidbit, which falls into the too-good-to-be-true category. In approximately 2006, Karen and I along with her cousin and husband were in Las Vegas to take in the first two days of the NCAA men's basketball tournament. In a break from the non-stop hoops action, Karen and her cousin ventured over to the Forum Shoppes at Caesar's Palace.

Rose was a frequent guest at a memorabilia shop there. Karen saw Pete, bought a memento (required) for him to sign and had a brief conversation. When she told the all-time hit king this was for her husband, Rose asked, "Well, where is he?" When Karen responded that I was over at the Bellagio watching and betting on the tourney games, the immediate response from Rose: "I wish I was there with him."

Special Day on All Counts

If you need a little more convincing that I'm all Reds fan all the time, how about this one:

October 20, 1990 was the date chosen for the marriage of my high school friend Steve Kinnett and his wife Nancy. It also happened to be the day of the fourth game of the 1990 World Series between the beloved Reds and the Oakland A's. (In 1972, the underdog A's defeated the Reds behind the likes of Joe Rudi, Sal Bando and Gene Tenace. This time around the script was flipped, with Oakland heavily favored with 12 more regular season wins and its third straight World Series appearance).

At a still young 28 years old, I was convinced there was a way to celebrate the special occasion and witness what could be the Series-clinching victory for the Reds. As I was in my sportswriting days in Anderson, I had to cover a high school football game that Friday night.

After fulfilling my responsibilities, I got in the car and drove to Cleveland to meet another friend on the way to Rochester, New York, for the wedding. The ceremony was beautiful, of course, but the reception did coincide with game time. No worries: A small, portable TV would allow me to take part in both.

Of course, many friends I grew up with – who were also Reds fans – were also eager to follow the baseball action. The small TV attracted quite a crowd. When the Reds pulled off the sweep with a 2-1 win behind the pitching of Series MVP Jose Rijo, we naturally celebrated by tracking down some brooms and waving them for all to see. I was kindly, but firmly, reminded by the groom's father that it was fine to be happy about the win but no more brandishing the brooms.

The Big Red Machine provided
plenty of reading material for fans of all ages.

A family friend provided tickets to
Game 1 of the 1970 World Series,
which I attended as an 8-year-old.

Pete Rose, despite his later gambling
troubles, was an early role model for
his play on the field.

CHAPTER 12

Beginning the Baseball Journey

I shared in the introduction that the first date for Karen and I was at the Reds Opening Day game in 1983. That was the first of many, many games we would attend together.

Karen grew up on the south side of Chicago. While my hometown of St. Leon boasted about 600 residents, her high school graduating class was more than 1,000. Despite the south side address, she was a diehard Cubs (and Bears, Blackhawks and Bulls) fan. An annual trip or two to Wrigley Field became commonplace.

As our family grew (daughter Megan born in 1991 and son Josh adopted in 2000), family vacations sometimes allowed visits to other cities and stadiums. There was San Francisco and San Diego in 2005 during a trip down the California coast. A journey East five years later coincided with games in New York (Mets) and Philadelphia.

It was shortly after that when we determined: Why not try to see a game in all 30 major league stadiums? They were fairly easy at first – a long weekend to Detroit and Cleveland in 2012, or the next year pairing Milwaukee and the Chicago White Sox on consecutive days.

Some of the others in ensuing years came together this way:
- Yankee Stadium on a Friday night before a Labor Day weekend at the U.S. Open tennis tournament (more on that sport later).
- A natural Baltimore-Washington combo.
- A 2019 three-games-in three-days scenario in Anaheim, Los Angles and Arizona. The ballgames were preceded by a day at Disneyland. And since the

schedule didn't cooperate, we actually went to Dodger Stadium on a Sunday, drove to Phoenix for Arizona (and the Dodgers) on Monday and returned to Anaheim for Angels-Reds on Tuesday.

- Arlington Stadium in Texas was a one-off to see the Cubs open the 2019 season at the Rangers. That also happened to be NCAA Elite Eight weekend, so I watched on phones/iPads at the ballpark with another Purdue fan as the Boilermakers fell short of the Final Four with an overtime loss to eventual campion Virginia.
- St. Louis was also a special one-city trip. It was Game 2 of the 2015 playoff series between Karen's Cubs and the Cardinals. A pair of key bunts (back when that was still a key part of the game) led to a Chicago victory.
- COVID won out in 2021 and the following year was limited to one game in Minnesota as we were undergoing a series of life changes – college graduation, wedding, retirement and moving to Arizona.
- It was time to wrap up this journey in 2022 this way: Kansas City (paired with another sporting event); Seattle and Oakland (and another unique sports opportunity); and finally Atlanta, Tampa and Miami before and after a Florida-based cruise.

Did we put together scrapbooks or keep notes about our adventure? No. But we almost always arrived early to walk around and take in sights both outside the stadiums and within the gates. We would seek out local food favorites – I more than Karen – and talk to other fans about their hometown ballparks and teams.

The memories are many. Among them (pre-2022 with that year covered later):

- Favorite stadiums: Karen immediately goes to the classics with Wrigley Field (1914) and Fenway Park (1912, more on Fenway immediately below). I have to add in San Francisco with its setting along the Bay. Many have seen images of the kayakers in right field's McCovey Cook waiting to race to those home run balls that exit AT&T Park, but inside during batting practice fans come with their own creative rope-and-bucket systems to scoop up batting practice balls that land near the outfield wall.
- Special weekend: When the 2017 schedule came out and late April dates were set for a Cubs visit to Boston, Chicago fans across the country jumped into action. Our flight from Indianapolis featured so many fans that Southwest Airlines pumped in the Go Cubs Go! victory song over the sound system.

On that flight and once in Beantown, we met so many supporters – some who had tickets to a game or games and many others who just wanted to experience the rare series between the two teams with the shared history of classic home fields and recently ended infamously long streaks without a world championship.

Boston's 2004 sweep of St. Louis (after coming back from a 3-0 deficit against the rival Yankees in the AL Championship series) was its first title since 1918. Chicago, of course, had ended an incredible 108-year drought less than six months earlier by capturing the 2016 World Series by winning the final three games against Cleveland.

The weekend was like a group therapy session. Boston fans, known in part for their surliness, could not have been nicer. Police on the streets were congratulating Cubs fans for finally putting an end to their decades of misery.

We did a bicycle tour of the city on Friday. One of the guides was a man who said he came from a small town in Indiana that you probably never heard of before my earlier mention. It was Knightstown, home of the Hoosier Gym. It was two years prior to my story on basketball in Henry County, but I was well aware of the community and the home court of the Hickory Huskers from *Hoosiers*.

By the way, bike tours are a great way to get a behind-the-scenes look at places you might be visiting for the first time. On non-baseball trips, we have enjoyed wonderful pedaling experiences in Washington, D.C.; Barcelona, Spain; and Melbourne, Australia among other places.

Fenway Park has to be the major league park that sits on the smallest plot of land. I don't know if the city grew around the ballpark or if Fenway was crammed into an existing space. It's not a complaint, just an observation. History oozes out of every nook and cranny, inside and out. We attended the Saturday and Sunday games, with the latter seats in right center field actually pointing directly toward first base. It took a turn of the body, or at least the head, to get a direct look at home plate.

The teams split the two games we saw, but the outcome was secondary. The experience was most memorable.

- Better than expected: We will throw five venues into this category (in no particular order). They are Baltimore (including markers with all the details of the longest home run balls); San Diego (like Baltimore, built to accompany existing brick business buildings); Pittsburgh (panoramic view of downtown after walking across the Roberto Clemente Bridge to reach PNC Park); Minnesota (simply a nice setting with great views); and Colorado (lots of enthusiasm in a vibrant downtown setting). The latter, by the way, is the only stadium Karen and I did not visit together with each taking in a game in conjunction with work conferences.

- Not what you see on TV: Los Angeles area fans won't like this, but the Dodger Stadium and Anaheim Stadium backdrops are deceiving. They are the third and fourth oldest major league stadiums, opening in 1962 and 1966, respectively. The picturesque mountains beyond center field in LA are much more evident at home than the wooden, worn bleachers in the outfield and the narrow passageways in other areas. Anaheim Stadium has a big rock formation in the outfield that you see on TV and that's about it. It is a somewhat dreary setting inside and out. Although when we were there, an enthusiastic throng of Japanese fans (about 80 in a group) cheered everything Shohei Ohtani did, then filed out when he batted for what appeared to be the last time in the seventh inning.
- Not high on the list: On the team's web site, Nationals Park (2008) is described this way: "The new park not only redefines modern sports facility architecture but also serves as the catalyst and cornerstone of a new mixed-use Capitol Riverfront in our nation's capital." We were not impressed (but again, see below). Arizona, closest to our new home as of 2021, Houston and Milwaukee (except for the extensive football-like tailgating) just seem to be there. Maybe it has to do with the roofs that are often closed.
- Barking up the right tree: When I purchased the tickets for Washington (on the back end of a Friday-Saturday doubleheader that started in Baltimore), I had no idea it was a special night at the ballpark. It became evident as we waited to enter that many four-legged friends would be joining us for Bark in the Park. And, in fact, we joined them when our rare outfield seats (I usually look initially down either the first or third base lines) were in the same section as the dogs. Karen, one of the biggest dog lovers I have ever known, made many new friends that night. Kirk Cousins, at the time the starting quarterback for the then Washington Redskins, sat nearby with his pup.
- Historically speaking: Some stadiums, not all, pay tribute to their history with various displays and exhibits. During our early visits, nothing came close to matching the Yankees and their celebration of the team's 27 World Series titles and 61 Hall of Fame players. Cleveland and Arizona were two others with impressive presentations.
- On the field: A September 2016 shootout between AL East contenders Boston and Toronto featured eight home runs and 18 pitchers. We were in Canada to attend the wedding of Karen's cousin, Julie, and her husband Michael (now our Arizona "neighbors" for half the year). Thanks for scheduling the nuptials for Monday.

- August 2014, Chris Heisey of the Reds hit two home runs in a 3-2 victory at Pittsburgh as Reds starter Johnny Cueto won his 16th game of the year. On a less positive note for Cincinnati, a 2010 trip to Citi Field saw the Mets' Johan Santana twirl a three-hit shutout and slam the only home run of his career.
- Filling the pallet: No trip to the ballpark is complete without some food – and it can't always be a hot dog or Cracker Jacks. Karen said nothing can beat Citi Field for its wide variety, including fresh salads. Garlic fries in San Francisco were a big hit for me, and the crab cakes in Baltimore did not disappoint.

Chicago to Houston

A couple of last notes on the baseball front:

I worked with and knew more than my share of Cubs fans. An annual trip to Wrigley Field for a summer afternoon contest often found me the only non-Cub fan on the journey (although I did back the North Siders if they weren't playing the Reds). When the two matched up, I was at a severe numbers disadvantage.

In August 2017, that was the case with the Reds scoring nine runs in the second inning off Cubs' ace Jon Lester. I apparently started celebrating a little too soon as Karen banished me from my seat to sit with some of the others in the group. The tide quickly turned as Chicago used six homers to eventually tie the game. Thankfully, for me, Cincinnati managed to pull out a 13-10 win.

In addition to the current stadium quest, Karen and I were able to attend several games at the Houston Astrodome, often billed as the Eighth Wonder of the World. Karen's parents had moved from Chicago to southeastern Texas in 1983. She gained her Cub allegiances from her father, Gordon. At one game that the three of us went to in the late 1980s, the Cubs' Greg Maddux was locked in a pitchers' duel. I believe the teams had combined for one hit through the first six innings of scoreless tie.

Gordon, a very early riser and always anxious to beat the traffic home, asked if we were ready to leave at that point. We did manage to stay a few more innings (not sure about the outcome of that game), but it spawned the joke that has lived on ever since: If Gordon went to a doubleheader, he would have to leave early twice.

On the road in Anaheim (top left), Baltimore (top right), Washington (bottom left) and Minneapolis.

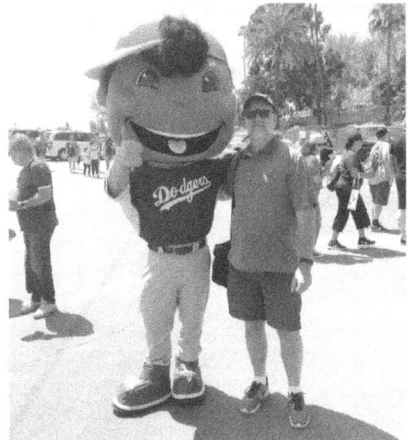

Fenway Park was a special destination, while I had the opportunity to pose with
a mascot at Dodger Stadium.

CHAPTER 13

Ruling the Jungle

The Cincinnati Reds are the oldest franchise in major league baseball, dating back to 1869. Ninety-nine years later, in 1968 when I was six years old, the Cincinnati Bengals played their first game in the American Football League (AFL).

My first memory of the team came a year later as quarterback Greg Cook (who played at the University of Cincinnati) appeared to be on the way to stardom. In leading the second-year franchise to a 3-0 start, Cook felt a pop in his shoulder. He missed three games, but the torn rotator cuff injury was not diagnosed. Cook came back to finish the season and was even named AFL Rookie of the Year.

Surgery after the season also revealed a partially detached biceps muscle. He never returned to form. The injury was similar to one suffered by Drew Brees in his last year in San Diego in 2005. He recovered and went on to many excellent years in New Orleans.

In year three (the first year after the NFL-AFL merger), the Bengals actually won the title in the new AFC Central division. After a 1-6 start, they won seven in a row before being shutout against Baltimore in the first round of the playoffs.

It's pretty easy to fast forward through most years of the team's nondescript history. I had the opportunity to attend a few games, but most of the fandom was limited to disappointing Sunday afternoons in front of the TV.

That changed, at least for one season, in 1981. I was a sophomore at Ball State, but it was still possible to watch most games as the Baltimore Colts were three years away from moving to Indianapolis and taking over the airwaves in the Hoosier state. My older brother, along with several cousins and friends from St. Leon, were Bengals season ticket holders. I was able to go to a couple of home games at Riverfront Stadium when others were unable to attend.

On January 3, 1982, I was among 55,420 on hand to see the Bengals hold off Buffalo, 28-21, in the first round of the playoffs. One of the memories from that day was very mild temperatures (near 70 degrees) for the third day of January.

Winter break was over, and I was back in Muncie after that when the weather turned more customary for the season. A little bit of snow as I recall, but extremely bitter temps as the week wore on. San Diego was coming to Cincinnati the following Sunday for the AFC Championship. At least two of the normal ticketholders in my brother's group opted out of what became known as the "Freezer Bowl".

What constitutes a Freezer Bowl? How about minus nine degrees air temperature with a wind chill of 59 below for the coldest game in NFL history. Colder than the more famous Ice Bowl (-13 and -48, respectively), the 1967 NFL championship between Green Bay and Dallas. Forrest Gregg, an offensive lineman for the Packers in that game, was now the Bengals coach.

I may have set a record for layers of clothing and even borrowed a snowsuit for further protection. It was a little difficult to recognize others as leaving skin exposed was an invitation to frostbite. One friend in our group, however, was easy to keep track of based on the expansive icicles dangling from his beard.

There were no drinks or other concessions available as basically everything was frozen. There were about 9,000 fewer fans than the week before. The opposing Chargers played in Miami a week earlier, winning in overtime in 84-degree heat that left some players dehydrated. The always hard Astroturf surface at Riverfront had to feel a bit like concrete in the conditions.

The Bengals may have won the game mentally when their offensive and defensive linemen came out in shirt sleeves. There was also a strategic element as players were allowed to apply Vaseline to protect exposed skin. Dave Lapham, a guard on that team and still a radio analyst, said, "We loaded our arms up. That was an advantage when defenders tried to swipe at you and grab your arms."

The Bengals won going away, 27-7, and were headed to the Super Bowl. It was much warmer in northern California later that afternoon when Dwight Clark made "The Catch" for San Francisco against Dallas to send the 49ers to their first Super Bowl.

Super Sunday

Most of the 15 previous Super Bowls to that point had taken place in Los Angeles, Miami or New Orleans. But in the happiest of coincidences, Super Bowl XVI had been awarded to the Pontiac Silverdome in the Detroit suburbs. Thus, my Bengals would be about a five-hour drive away on January 24, 1982, as they sought the Super Bowl title.

In February 2022, limited face value tickets for the Super Bowl were priced at just under $1,000. On the resale market, however, those tickets were closer to the $3,000 range before additional fees were added in. Forty years earlier, the NFL made tickets available for $40. And most of the season ticket group of family and friends were able to secure those tickets.

My focus was supposed to be on college. But I had the best parents in the world. I noted earlier my father's support of the Reds. In addition, I was with my mom at Riverfront Stadium for the 1970 World Series game and the Seaver no-hitter eight years later. They helped their financially challenged son pay $125 to a ticket broker in Cincinnati in order to attend the Big Game.

Five of us, my brother included, headed north on Interstate 75 the day before the game. Yes, we were headed inside the next day for the game, but it was January in Michigan. Not Freezer Bowl temps and wind chill, but plenty of snow on the ground and about 30 below wind chill on the walk from the parking lot to the Silverdome. Undoubtedly, that was part of the reason we did not see another cold weather Super Bowl until more than 20 years later.

My ticket was separate from the others, so I had the "opportunity" to make new friends. That wasn't easy as the Bengals came out with the proverbial "deer in the headlights" look and fell behind 20-0 at halftime. They did battle back, losing 26-21, but the outcome could have been different if not for a third quarter goal line stand in which the Bengals were stopped on four plays from inside the five.

I was seated in the last row of the lower bowl (a very good seat) and remember the halftime show was the popular (at the time) Up With People. We hopped in the van, drove back to Cincinnati and lamented the missed opportunities. I then made the two-hour drive back to Ball State and was in my seat for my 9 a.m. Monday class.

Coming Up Short

Joe Montana, a college standout at Notre Dame, was the quarterback for San

Francisco in that first Super Bowl. He was in that same role seven years later when the two teams met in the Super Bowl in Miami. I watched that one from our apartment in Anderson.

The Bengals took a late lead in a low-scoring game, then watched Montana take his team 93 yards in the final minute. Jerry Rice, the greatest wide receiver of all time, was unstoppable but the winning TD pass in the last minute went to his running mate John Taylor. In what may only be a slight exaggeration, Karen says I was still staring at the TV a few hours later wondering what had happened.

The Bengals won a playoff game in 1991, then became irrelevant for the next decade and a half. I still frequently wore a Bengals jacket I had and took the abuse from a series of seasons that often included only three or four wins. The "Bungles" nickname attached to my team did wear thin quickly.

The bright spot during these lean years was having the opportunity to attend a few Bengals games with a good friend who grew up in Cincinnati and just happened to be the math department chair at Ball State. It's really not an exaggeration to say Dale Umbach (and his family) bled black and orange. After suffering for so long, I'm sad that Dale was not there for the 2021-2022 run to the Super Bowl. But I'm sure he was enjoying it from above with a big smile on his face.

The conclusion of the 2005 season was particularly painful. Cincinnati ended a 14-year streak of losing seasons by winning the division. But coming to town for the first round of the playoffs was archrival Pittsburgh. For so many years, the Steelers had not only been the antithesis of the Bengals as far as on-field success and fan support, but they had come to Cincinnati on a regular basis and made it their "home".

Steeler fans were notorious for traveling to opposing cities in droves and waving their Terrible Towels. I respected them for their loyalty and dedication but couldn't stand their dominance of the Bengals. It was just about to get worse.

Carson Palmer, whose 32 TD passes that year led the NFL, fired a 66-yard strike to Chris Henry for a score on the Bengals' first possession. The celebration was short-lived as Palmer was hit low by a former Cincinnati defensive lineman and suffered a gruesome knee injury. Predictably, Pittsburgh went on to a 31-17 victory.

There were actually some good-natured Steeler fans in our section of the stadium. When I told them I was living in Indianapolis, they said, "See you next week when we come play the Colts."

I'm confident that same crew was on hand – as I was – for another wild game. The Colts were favored by two touchdowns. There wasn't huge concern the day of the game when the Colts learned that defensive back Nick Harper had been stabbed with a steak knife by his wife in a domestic dispute the night before.

Pittsburgh dominated most of the game before the Colts closed to within three points late in the contest. The Steelers are running out the clock when running back Jerome "The Bus" Bettis (a Notre Dame product) uncharacteristically fumbles near the Indianapolis goal line.

None other than Harper scooped up the ball and raced down the field. Whether it was the stabbing from the night before or divine intervention, something slowed down Harper enough for lumbering Steeler QB Ben Roethlisberger to make an ankle tackle and save the touchdown. The Colts moved downfield to set up a tying field goal, but kicker Mike Vanderjagt booted one of the ugliest kicks of all time. The Steelers won in Denver the next week and earned the franchise's fifth Super Bowl title by defeating Seattle in the Super Bowl at Ford Field in Detroit (same city, different location than the first Bengal Super Bowl loss in 1982).

There were just too many coincidences and fluke plays throughout that postseason. It was most frustrating for the Bengals to lose that opening game – and equally maddening to see the Steelers win again.

What soon followed was the most successful – and depressing – stretch in Bengals history. Six playoff appearances in seven years from 2009-2015 with no January wins to show for it. Here were the games (I attended the first four):

- 24-14 at home in 2009 to a Jets team that barely made the playoffs. Shayne Graham missed two relatively short field goals and Palmer threw for a pedestrian 146 yards while completing half of his passes. While exiting Paul Brown Stadium, a Palmer jersey came floating down from the skies above – a sign that at least one Bengals fan had reached his or her end point.
- 31-10 and 19-13 in back-to-back losses in Houston in 2011-12. With high school friend Kirk Gutzwiller living nearby, it was an easy trip for me. Not so much for the team. In the first game, third-string quarterback T.J. Yates (who, you rightfully ask) led the Texans. In the second, the Bengals never threw a first-half pass in the direction of leading receiver A.J. Green.
- 27-10 at home to San Diego in 2013. The home team, for some inexplicable reason, was never competitive
- 26-10 in Indianapolis in 2014. The game was about 11 miles from my house, but I had no desire to make the short trip. Our family had attended the regular season game between the two teams, in which the Bengals ran 27 plays on nine consecutive three-and-out drives in the first half.

- And if all that wasn't enough, 18-16 at home to Pittsburgh in 2015 in one of the greatest giveaways of all time. The Bengals fumbled the ball away while running out the clock, then committed consecutive personal foul penalties to put the Steelers in position for a chip shot winning field goal. Karen declined to stay in the same room with me while watching at home, and son Josh worried about my ability to cope with that defeat.

A Miracle Season

The next five years were primarily a return to the vast wasteland of most of the 1990s and early 2000s. I still attended a few games, wore the jerseys and absorbed the losses. The expectations, however, were quite low. That began to change in 2020 after drafting LSU quarterback Joe Burrow with the No. 1 pick. After a promising start, it was no surprise when Burrow was done for the season with a serious knee injury suffered on a sack against Washington.

Burrow was back at full strength for 2021. Known for their stinginess over the years, the franchise had invested in its defense through free agency. Cautious optimism was the feeling entering the season.

The record was 7-6 through 13 games. Despite our move that summer to Arizona, we managed to attend two games. A return to Cincinnati in late September for a beloved uncle's funeral coincided with a Thursday night home against Jacksonville. The Bengals did not play well, leading only on the last play of the game – a field goal from rookie kicker Evan McPherson.

In November, the Bengals just happened to be playing in Las Vegas on an already planned trip for us. McPherson booted three field goals from beyond 50 yards in a 32-13 victory. Still, there were four home losses as of mid-December and work to do to even make the playoffs.

A win at Denver came first. Then a 41-21 thrashing of Baltimore the day after Christmas gave the Bengals sweeps of both the Ravens and Steelers with a winning margin of 89 points in the four games. The division was clinched with an improbable 34-31 come-from-behind victory at home against the defending AFC champion Kansas City Chiefs.

My team was back in the playoffs but there was that disturbing history. The last playoff win was so long ago – after the 1990 season – that it came against the Houston Oilers (a name which had not even existed for the past 25 years).

First up is a rematch with the Raiders. Overcoming a pedigree of finding a way to lose when it mattered most, the Bengals made enough big plays to win 26-19. Then it was on the road against AFC top seed Tennessee. McPherson nailed four field goals for the second week in a row, including a game-winning 52-yarder on the final play.

I watched nervously on the back porch of our Arizona home. The outside viewing allowed plenty of room for pacing and a little yelling during both contests. Following the game, Kirk in Texas called with a proposal for he and his wife to come to Arizona prior to the Super Bowl. If the Bengals happened to be there in Los Angeles, we might consider making the six-hour drive.

But there was an obstacle remaining in those Kansas City Chiefs, who roared to a 21-3 (remember that score) first-half lead in the AFC Championship. Three weeks earlier, the Bengals had trailed the Chiefs by 14 at home. But this was in KC and the Chiefs were simply marching up and down the field.

The final 65 seconds of the half were crucial as I continued the back-porch nervousness. The Bengals scored on a 41-yard screen pass, then stopped the Chiefs inside the 5-yard line on the final play. A 21-10 deficit at least offered hope.

Just like the regular season game, the Cincinnati defense dominated in the second half with the Chief scoring only three points. Kansas City won the overtime toss, but a quick interception and some key pass plays set up McPherson's winning kick.

Bengals 27, Chiefs 24. WOW! I think I managed to wipe away a few tears before anyone noticed. But there was no removing the smile from my face or the satisfaction of knowing that my team would be playing in the final game of the season. The phone messages and texts from family and friends flowed quickly.

Those feelings multiplied in the two weeks leading up to the Super Bowl. As I rolled out a long line of Cincinnati shirts, hats and jerseys, there was a near universal voicing of support for the underdog Bengals. Oh sure, there was the pickleball pal (you know who you are) who said upon seeing the Burrow jersey on the courts the day after the KC game, "I don't have to look at that sh-- for the next two weeks, do I?"

But my team was seemingly America's team – at least for one game. Kirk and wife Betty made the trip from Texas, but we weren't ready to pay that $3,000 plus just for tickets. The porch TV had worked well for three weeks, so why not stick with it? A few more nearby friends came over – maybe more to watch me and my reactions than the game.

Yes, the Bengals lost 23-20 to the home team Rams on a touchdown with 1:25 left. It was a final drive reminiscent of Joe Montana and the 49ers 33 years earlier.

A win, of course, was the ultimate prize. But I felt mostly content. It was such a remarkable run from nowhere to near championship.

Son Josh, who seemingly solidified his Bengal fandom during his time at the University of Cincinnati, called visibly upset and asked how I was able to cope with the previous losses. I mumbled something wise about defeats becoming easier as you mature.

An RCA Dome Memory

I mentioned earlier to remember that 21-3 score. Somewhere high on the top 10 list of all-time sports events attended was another game that featured that same score. It was in January 2007, the year after watching both the Bengals and Colts lose to the Steelers.

This time it was an AFC Championship matchup between the Colts and their dreaded playoff rivals – the New England Patriots. The two teams had dominated the AFC in recent years, but the Patriots had dominated when the games mattered most. While Karen and I were still cheering on the Bears and Bengals first, the Colts in our adopted hometown had certainly become our "second team".

We secured four tickets for the heavily anticipated matchup. Karen and Megan were in a lower section near my brother and sister-in-law. Josh and I (and several friends) were in the second row from the top in some partially obstructed seats.

Colts' fans were expecting a victory. Patriot fans had all the laughs, and the vocal jabs our way, in the first half as they built a 21-0 advantage. An Indianapolis field goal made the score 21-3 at the half. When the kick sailed through the uprights, 7-year-old Josh asked me if he could give it to the Patriot fans. I advised him to wait.

The Colts took their only lead late on an 80-yard touchdown drive before Marlin Jackson intercepted a Tom Brady pass to seal the victory. It was an electric atmosphere inside the old RCA Dome before the game, in the early going and especially during the second-half rally. And yes, Josh did get to "give it" to the Patriot fans who good-naturedly took the jabs.

The Colts' comeback from the 21-3 deficit was the largest in a conference final in NFL history. It was matched by the Bengals in 2021.

With Karen's Chicago roots (the Colts did defeat the Bears in that 2007 Super Bowl), there were also some several interesting contests involving the Bears. A few of the highlights:

• Several trips to Soldier Field for Bears-Bengals games. At one, a Bears fans sitting behind us in the stands shared this analysis with Karen – "What are you doing with him? He must have money" – as the man noticed my Cincinnati jersey and hat. At a separate game, we walked through the tailgate area and a passionate Chicago fan advised I move along quickly before he got the bow and arrow out from the back of his pickup. I thought he was kidding, but wasn't sure, so I did move along quickly.

- Two Bears-Lions games in Detroit. The first was a mid-1980s contest at the Silverdome where I had witnessed Super Bowl XVI. The struggling Lions had a crowd of less than 30,000 the week before against Atlanta. The crowd more than doubled seven days later with Detroit becoming Chicago East. Many years later, Ford Stadium was the venue for a Bears-Lions Thanksgiving tradition. The home team rallied to win that one.
- Finally, as a Bears fan, Karen does not like (to say it mildly) the rival Green Bay Packers. It's very similar to the way to I feel about the Steelers. But as a true sports fan, she also recognized the lure of legendary Lambeau Field. And if we were going to make the trip there, we reasoned we might as well go all in – as in mid-December of 2019 with temperatures in the single digits and snow on the ground. As in Boston two years earlier with Red Sox-Cubs, the fans couldn't have been nicer. Green Bay was the winner, but it was another special day.

An office takeover at the Indiana Chamber allowed me to showcase some Bengals' paraphernalia.

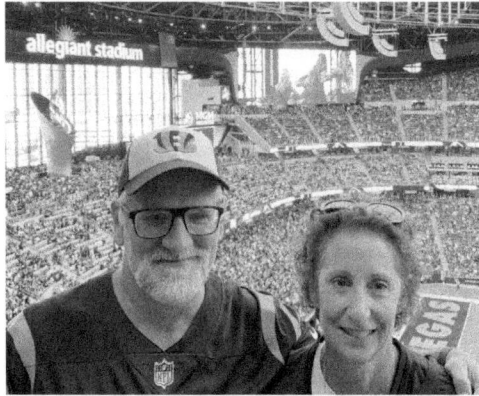

A visit to Las Vegas in 2021 to see the Bengals against the Raiders in Allegiant Stadium.

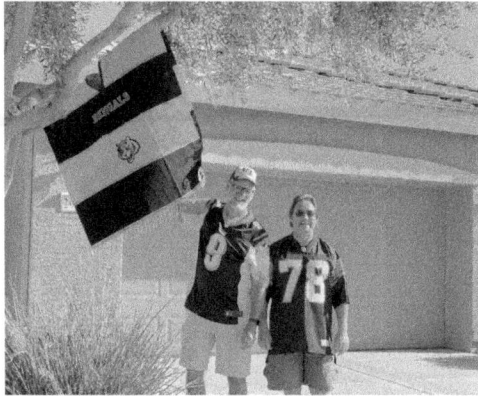

Super Bowl morning in Arizona in 2022 with good friend Kirk Gutzwiller.

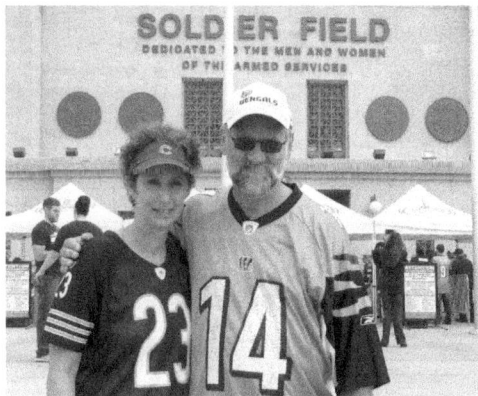

Enjoying one of several excursions to Soldier Field in Chicago, where my Bengals' gear proved unpopular.

CHAPTER 14

Bulldog Power

A common question for someone with my affliction: What is your favorite sport?

Forced to pick one, I would go with college basketball. The on-campus atmosphere can't be beat. Defense is a constant (as opposed to the professional game) and each game carries a certain significance. It's good on TV – and it's even better in person when teams play the game the way it is supposed to be played.

That's exactly what Butler University did, starting in the early 2000s. A small private school just north of downtown Indianapolis, Butler possessed a solid, but unspectacular, basketball tradition. That changed as a series of coaches emphasized "The Butler Way," a complete commitment to teamwork above all else.

The Bulldogs earned two Sweet Sixteen berths as part of six NCAA Tournament appearances in the first decade of the 21st century. In addition, its home games were at Hinkle Fieldhouse, the largest college basketball arena in the county for several decades from its completion in 1928. Resembling an old barn, Hinkle's sunlight shining through the windows on a Saturday afternoon was – and still is – an experience to remember.

Hinkle was the longtime home of the Indiana high school state championships and served as the scene for the final game in the movie *Hoosiers*. Now living in Indianapolis, we began attending a few Butler games in addition to trips to Muncie to see Ball State play. Part of it, for me, was jealousy. Butler competed on a consistent basis the way I wish Ball State did.

Thad Matta, the Hoopeston high school star I followed as a reporter at my first job in Illinois, was the Butler coach in 2000. He left for greener pastures at Xavier. Todd Lickliter followed with six solid seasons before departing for Iowa. Brad Stevens took over in 2007 at the age of 30.

Stevens, listed at 6-foot-1, had played guard at nearby Zionsville High School and Division III DePauw University. He was on a career path with Indianapolis-based Eli Lilly and Company, one of the leading pharmaceutical companies in the world, when he opted to return to basketball as a volunteer coach with the Bulldogs. He was a full-time assistant for five years before ascending to the top role.

Two-thirds of the players on the Bulldog roster in 2009-10 played at Indiana high schools. Matt Howard was an undersized 6-foot-8 center from Connersville (my East Central teams played there in the high school days) who made up for any size shortcomings with hustle and determination. Gordon Hayward, a 6-9 sophomore from Brownsburg (five miles from my current home on the west side of Indianapolis) was a talented guard-forward with a strong all-around game.

Butler went 8-4 in the nonconference season, losing to ranked teams Minnesota, Clemson and Georgetown in neutral court games. A December 22 loss at UAB was the fourth setback – and the last one until early April.

The Bulldogs proceeded to win 18 straight Horizon League games, 12 of them by double digits. It's never easy to win against familiar opponents (Loyola, Wisconsin-Milwaukee and Detroit among them) on their home court, but Butler pulled off the feat to move as high as No. 10 in the national rankings.

At 26-4, the Bulldogs assured themselves of an NCAA berth with conference tourney wins over Wisconsin-Milwaukee and Wright State. Earning a best-ever No. 5 seed, Butler went west to San Jose and picked up NCAA tourney victories over No. 12 UTEP and No. 13 Murray State (the latter by two points).

Top seed Syracuse was the next victim (in Salt Lake City), sending Butler to its first Elite Eight. Now is where it gets a little tricky for me. The Schumans (with another family and high school friends of our daughter Megan) are leaving two days later on a spring break cruise. That is the day of the next game against No. 2 seed Kansas State.

Fortunately, we are onboard and taking over the sports bar. We meet a few more Butler fans along the way and outnumber the Kansas State faithful by approximately 20 to 1. The Bulldogs fall behind late, 52-51, but go on a 12-2 run and end up with a 63-56 win. We have a week on a cruise to celebrate, but also plan for the Final Four, which just happens to be in Indianapolis.

I already had two tickets to the Final Four through the lottery. Friends on the cruise were Butler ticketholders and worked their connections to secure two more. But there were some logistical challenges to get from Miami, Florida, to Indianapolis, Indiana on Saturday, April 3.

Here's how it eventually worked: The cruise ship docking early that morning in Miami. A bus ride to Fort Lauderdale to catch a flight. A stop in Charlotte before ending up in Louisville, about 120 miles south of Indianapolis, where several cars were parked.

Friend Scott and I, along with our sons, were going to the lucky ones going to the semifinal games. Which means we have the best wives ever. Not only did Karen give up her ticket for Josh, but she and the others volunteered to wait for our luggage and drive most of the crew home. The four of us, with daughter Megan (somebody had to drive my car home from outside Lucas Oil Stadium because there would be no time to find a parking spot), sped off as soon as we could.

When I say sped, I mean it. It was after 4:00 when we left Louisville with game time at 6:00. We darted around and through some traffic issues. In a surreal scene, we pulled off the interstate just south of Indianapolis to literally grab Scott's two tickets from a friend waiting on the side of the road. We navigated the rest of the trip, pulled onto a side street near the stadium, turned my keys over to Megan and the four of us walked in as the National Anthem was being played.

Josh and I were in the upper deck, surrounded by fans from various parts of the country. All were rooting for the underdog Bulldogs to continue their magical ride. They did with a bruising 52-50 win over Michigan State, the fifth straight tournament game in which they held their opponent under 60 points. Losing coach Tom Izzo said of the Bulldogs, "I like the way they play. I like their story. They play like a Big Ten team."

Butler became the smallest school to play for the national title in 40 years. And it was doing so in its hometown. On Monday, several Bulldogs attended class before returning downtown to prepare to play one of the game's bluebloods – the Duke Blue Devils. There appeared to be a few thousand Duke fans amidst 70,000-plus hoping for Butler to complete its Cinderella ride.

Megan got the second ticket this time (both kids should thank their mom again). We returned to the same seats and witnessed an instant classic. If you are a basketball fan at all, you already know how the game ended – a halfcourt shot by Hayward that caromed off the backboard and rim before falling harmlessly to the floor in a 61-59 Duke victory. An ESPN analysis found that the shot missed by three inches.

A short fadeaway baseline jumper by Hayward had just bounced off the rim a few seconds earlier. Duke rebounded, made the first free throw and intentionally missed the second as Butler had no timeouts. Howard set a jarring screen to free Hayward for the shot that has been replayed in every NCAA tournament since. It's probably the most famous non-winning shot in basketball history. When I see the replays, I still carry this small bit of hope that it will go in this time.

Leaving the stadium that night, we were mostly in shock at what could have been – and the outstanding game we saw. Butler had gone toe-to-toe with the then four-time national champs. Butler's record 25-game winning streak was over, but it had won the hearts of the nation. President Obama called the team the next day to congratulate it on its outstanding performance.

Repeating the Near Miracle

The once-in-a-lifetime Butler story was repeated the following season. Two contributing seniors graduated, and Hayward departed early for the NBA. A 9-4 nonconference record was similar to the previous year. But a three-game losing streak left the Bulldogs 6-5 in the Horizon League in early February. The next loss, after 14 straight wins, was April 4 in Houston in the national title game against Connecticut.

As a No. 8 seed, the five NCAA tourney wins were by a combined 21 points. Karen and I were in Las Vegas for our near annual excursion to watch the opening days of the tournament. A last-second tip-in by Howard secured a 60-58 win over Old Dominion in the first round. Top regional seed Pittsburgh was next.

Watching the game from a Vegas sportsbook, we were next to some young Pittsburgh fans who were cheering for Butler to keep it close so they could win their bets in addition to their team advancing. We warned them of the flaws in that logic. Butler had a big early lead, came back from a second-half deficit and won when Howard was fouled with less than a second remaining.

Wisconsin and Florida were the next two victims, the second one in overtime. Incredibly, Butler was going back to the Final Four. And I was going to be there once again. Kirk, who would host me the next two years in Houston for those Bengal playoff losses, would this time welcome three of us who went to high school together.

Butler was not the Cinderella this time around as 11th-seeded Virginia Commonwealth had made its way from the First Four to the Final Four. The Bulldogs dispatched the Commodores 70-62 to return to the title game. There, they actually led by three at halftime but shot 19% overall in a 53-41 setback.

The outcome was disappointing, but the joy of having a "dog" in the fight so to speak was exhilarating. It was so much fun to make our way around the Houston area and meet Bulldog fans young and old. Butler has been to five NCAA tourneys since, advancing to the Sweet 16 once. It has struggled at times in the Big East Conference, a move made possible by its two-year run of excellence. Hinkle Fieldhouse remains a shrine for basketball fans.

Hinkle Magic

Three more quick items before leaving the Bulldogs behind.

1. Howard, the undersized center, made a play that symbolizes The Butler Way and what the program is all about. In 2011, the Bulldogs were leading visiting Stanford by more than 25 points in the second half. Chasing a loose ball, Howard dove off the court and made the save, leading to a basket. The score didn't matter. The fact that he was likely exiting the game soon wasn't a factor. My description doesn't do justice to the hustle and team-first mentality Howard displayed.

By the way, the Schumans were at that game after celebrating a family Christmas in St. Leon earlier in the day. We "invented" the Christmas brunch celebration in order to be able to make the two-hour drive back to Indianapolis for the afternoon contest.

2. In 2013, No. 13 Butler hosted No. 8 Gonzaga in an ESPN Gameday battle. It was another classic. Roosevelt Jones, a 6-foot-4 sophomore for Butler who may be the only college player I have seen who did not have any form of a jump shot, stole an inbound pass from 7-foot Zag center Kelly Olynyk with 3.5 seconds left, drove from center court and floated in a shot from the lane at the buzzer for a 64-63 victory. Josh tried to figure out how we could participate from the second level in one of the best court rushes I had seen, but we didn't make it.

3. Butler recorded back-to-back homecourt wins over top-ranked Villanova in 2017 and 2018. In the first of those games, Karen and I sat near some Wildcat fans with several young children. The kids were fighting back tears at the end of the upset loss, but when we offered consoling words to the parents, they responded that coming to Hinkle Fieldhouse was on their bucket list and they loved every moment of the experience despite the loss.

Hanging out with Hink, the Butler mascot, at the Maui Classic in Las Vegas in 2021.

Back-to-back trips to the NCAA title game put Butler on the basketball map.

Celebrating an upset of No. 1 Villanova at Hinkle Fieldhouse.

CHAPTER 15

The Road Ends Here

I f college basketball is my favorite sport (see previous chapter), then the Final Four has to be a desired destination. We've talked about Butler's magical two-year run in 2010 and 2011. I've been fortunate to have attended five Final Fours prior to that and most that have taken place since.

Getting there has proven to be far easier than trying to secure tickets to the Super Bowl. The system has evolved a bit over the years, but in general it works like this:

Submit an application online in the spring and pay for up to four tickets (reasonably priced, in my view, at just below or above $200 each for the package that includes the semifinals and championship). Resale tickets are another story that we'll get to shortly.

Learn from the NCAA in late August whether your application was selected in the lottery. A few months later, you are informed of your seat location. The good news is that you are in the building. The bad news is be prepared to supplement your on-court viewing with binoculars or glances at the big screen. Sure, the view is better on TV. But, just like other big events, you're there for the atmosphere and excitement.

Longtime best friends Kirk (the Texas connection), Dale (actually from St. Leon and living in the Memphis area in recent years) and I apply each year. And all but one time since 2011, at least one of us has been a lottery winner. So, our annual reunion takes place in various basketball-crazy cities across the country.

Early Final Fours for me were a result of living in Indianapolis, home of the NCAA headquarters (which moved from the Kansas City area in the late 1990s). A portion of the agreement for that transition included bringing both the men's and women's Final Fours to Indianapolis on a regular basis.

In 1997, Kirk and I enjoyed the first title for the Arizona Wildcats. After beating regional top seed Kansas on the way to Indianapolis, the Wildcats defeated two more No. 1's in North Carolina and Kentucky (in overtime). Guards Miles Simon and Mike Bibby led the way for Arizona.

Karen and I were on hand for two other RCA Dome title games – Michigan State (led by the Flint, Michigan trio of Mateen Cleaves, Morris Peterson and Charlie Bell) over Florida in 2000 and those Gators (Al Horford and Joakim Noah) topping UCLA six years later for the first of two back-to-back titles.

It's no secret why the Final Four, and other major sporting events, continue to return to Indianapolis. Simply put, the city knows its stuff as part of an amateur sports strategy that dates back to the 1970s. There is no shortage of enthusiastic and knowledgeable volunteers. Hotels, restaurants and other attractions are located downtown within walking distance.

Jim Nantz and Jay Bilas are among the commentators who have said they would have no problem if the Final Four was in Indy every year. But it's understandable why the NCAA moves the tournament – and the financial benefits it brings – to different parts of the country.

One destination that has not seen a Final Four return is the Tampa-St. Petersburg area. This was another Final Four experience, sort of, prior to 2010. The year was 1999. I secured two tickets through the lottery. But the games fell during spring break for 7-year-old Megan, and something didn't seem right about going to Florida without her. Thus, Steve (the Ball State-Anderson friend) went with us to use one of the tickets while Karen and I were to split the other.

Logistics were not an advantage for the Floridians. We stayed in Clearwater, our choice, so it was a healthy trip to Tampa where most of the festivities (coaches' meetings, fan events and more) took place. It was another 22 miles across the bay to St. Petersburgh and the dome (the home of the Tampa Bay Devil Rays and the place where we attended the Ball State bowl game years later).

Karen and Megan dropped Steve and I off in Tampa on their way to Disney World for the day on Saturday. We did run into Ball State coach Ray McCallum and had a nice talk about Cardinal prospects for the next few years. Later, we ended up having a beverage at a nearby bar that was home to many assistant coaches and others associated with college programs – big and small.

To make what could be a long story short, we sold our two tickets for that day for $1,000. It was a cash business with the "broker" tossing down 10 $100 bills out of a large roll in his pocket to complete the transaction. Steve and I assumed we might be able to purchase some better tickets prior to gametime.

Once we navigated our way to St. Petersburg on a bus we were not supposed to be on, we learned the going rate for tickets was even higher. Big schools Ohio State, Michigan State, Duke and Connecticut were preparing to play and plenty of other fans had also made their way to Florida.

We opted to watch on big screens in a tent outside the stadium. The crowds overwhelmed the organizers, but we enjoyed watching the Big Ten teams get sent home. Steve and Karen attended the Monday night final, where UConn topped Duke, while I viewed on TV from our home for the weekend.

The other pre-2010 Final Four had Dale and I making the trip to San Antonio in 2004 (they were Kirk's tickets, but he was working in the Philippines at the time).

More Final Four Experiences

We – Kirk, Dale and I – have enjoyed our Final Four get-togethers 10 times between 2011 and 2022. We did not get tickets for Atlanta in 2013, there was no tourney in 2020 due to COVID and the 2021 event (played in its entirety in Indiana) had very limited attendance.

Sometimes it is the three of us; other times, we are joined by additional friends. Our destinations have been Houston (2011 and 2016), New Orleans (2012 and 2022), Dallas area (2014), Indianapolis (2015), Phoenix (2017), San Antonio (2018) and Minneapolis (2019). Among the highlights, both on and off the court:

- New Orleans, 2012: Steve completed our quartet as his Kentucky team (he grew up a Wildcat fan in Evansville, Indiana) was the favorite to win. Led by three freshmen (Anthony Davis and Michael Kidd-Gilchrist among them) and two sophomores, Kentucky defeated archrival Louisville in the semifinals and Kansas in the championship to finish 38-2. Steve said the experience wiped out the pain from the overtime loss to Arizona 15 years earlier in Indianapolis.

Bourbon Street and some of the best seafood one can find help make New Orleans a very good host city. We also witnessed a Jimmy Buffet free concert that included New Orleans Saints coach Sean Payton, who had been suspended for his role in the Bountygate scandal.

- North Texas, 2014: We stayed a mile away from AT&T Stadium in Arlington. Miserable weather kept us from various outdoor activities. UConn, seeded seventh, defeated No. 8 Kentucky in the final behind Shabazz Napier. For the only the second time since 1973, there were no Indiana teams in the tourney.

- Indianapolis, 2015: Kentucky entered the Final Four at 38-0 but was knocked out by Wisconsin, which fell to Duke for the title. Karen joined the three of us, but our seats in the south end zone were a long way from the end of the court. We were used to being up high in the stands, but the hope is always to be on the sidelines and as near center court as possible.
- Houston, 2016: Great weather led to a fun day in Galveston on Sunday between games, where we saw Purdue coach Matt Painter among others. On the court, in one of the best finishes ever, Villanova's Kris Jenkins drilled a three-pointer at the buzzer to defeat North Carolina. Often overlooked is that the game was tied because the Tar Heels' Marcus Paige connected on a double clutch three-pointer with 4.7 seconds remaining.

The NCAA often provides championship game fans with seat cushions. The sheer drama of a buzzer beater to win the national title prompted thousands of those cushions to be sent flying. Great game. Great experience. A great time, as always.

- Phoenix, 2017: The Arizona Cardinals' home in Glendale was a first-time venue. Phoenix hosted the primary off-court events. Our trio stayed in Mesa with the father of one of my Indiana Chamber co-workers and good friends. People warned to stay away from the Phoenix traffic and Glendale, despite an entertainment complex set up to handle such events, seemed a bit overwhelmed by the crowds. But I loved my first trip to the Valley, not knowing it would be our new home four years later. The Final Four is returning there in 2024.

North Carolina gained revenge for its loss the year before with a 71-65 victory over Gonzaga, which made it to the final game of the season for the first time after nearly two decades of top rankings and outstanding play.

- San Antonio, 2018: No. 11 seed Loyola (Chicago) and Sister Jean, the team's 98-year-old team chaplain and chief cheerleader, were the story of the tourney. Fans gave Sister Jean a standing ovation when she was spotted along the Riverwalk prior to Saturday's games. I even bought a Loyola shirt the day before to show my support for the underdogs.

Loyola led Michigan throughout the first half before the Wolverines came back to win. But this was Villanova's tournament with big wins over Kansas (95-79) and Michigan (79-62).

- Minneapolis, 2019: The Metrodome had hosted Final Fours in 1992 and 2001. So, the city was not new to the role. An easy-to-use train system, and downtown collection of bars and restaurants was a good combination. Our special event on Sunday was a robotics shooting challenge between several universities (Purdue included) at a local high school. We had the chance to interact with special guests and NCAA hoops legends David Robinson and Christian Laettner.

Virginia (remember, I followed along while at a Cubs-Rangers game in Arlington as it broke the Boilermakers' hearts in an Elite Eight overtime) knocked off Texas Tech in an extra session for the championship. The Cavaliers were led by Kyle Guy, an Indiana high school product from the northeast side of Indianapolis.

- New Orleans, 2022: We added two newcomers (high school friends) as we returned to the Crescent City with a group of six. Same great local live music on Bourbon Street, a concert in the riverfront park that featured Imagine Dragons and Kansas coming back from a 15-point halftime deficit to defeat North Carolina were among the memories.

We hope to continue the Final Four tradition for years to come.

Trips to the Final Four are always special and have produced a number of interesting stories ... maybe for the next book.

Hats are always a potential Final Four souvenir.

CHAPTER 16

Love That Game

I mentioned early on that I played tennis in high school. There was no master plan leading up to that as I don't recall playing much, if at all, before then and was looking for a sport to participate in during the fall season. Recreational tennis continued in college and beyond. But the fact that Karen and I still possess Jack Kramer and Stan Smith model wooden rackets reveals that we haven't exactly stayed active in the sport.

Indianapolis, however, had a long history hosting professional tour events. In high school, that involved a trip to the capital city to see Jimmy Connors and others play on clay. Two decades later, that tourney was part of the summer hardcourt season leading up to the U.S. Open. Pete Sampras, Jim Courier, Andre Agassi and others were among the top players we saw play.

In August 1996, Karen and I were in the stands for a night match. Agassi was coming off recent wins in the Olympics and the ATP tourney in Cincinnati. After his serve was broken in the fifth game of the second set, Agassi launched a tennis ball into the stands, then reportedly cursed at the umpire. There was no immediate announcement as he left the court. Some fans threw various items and most booed. As tourney officials tried to reach a resolution (Agassi was disqualified), the cute dogs representing tourney sponsor RCA ran around the court. A highlight was one of the dogs deciding to relieve himself on the courtside flowers. But Agassi never returned, and we all went home unhappy.

Two years later, we were in the same facility as the United States hosted Belgium in a Davis Cup match. Many of the top U.S. players sat out the quarterfinal match, but the hosts were 4-1 winners behind Todd Martin. The enthusiastic and patriotic atmosphere was a welcome change from the normal quiet tennis environment.

For nearly 10 years, Karen and I volunteered (primarily as ushers) at the ATP tour stop. At that point, the tourney was two weeks or so after Wimbledon. Many of the top players did not participate, but it was popular among young Americans. Yes, we were doing our part to help out. But we were also taking advantage of the opportunity to witness some competitive play.

Primarily after the Indianapolis tourney was transferred to Atlanta, we switched to in-person viewing at the very popular Cincinnati tournament for men (and later) women. As a Masters 1000 event two weeks before the U.S. Open, nearly all the top players were competing. This was during the Roger Federer-Rafael Nadal-Novak Djokovic heyday.

The Big Four in tennis, however, are the majors. That's the Australian, French and U.S. Opens in addition to Wimbledon. We made it a goal to try and experience our own Grand Slam.

U.S. Open

The first stop was New York City in 2005. The best timeframe for us was the middle of the tournament over Labor Day weekend. We took the purple No. 7 subway from the city to Flushing Meadow (Friday and Saturday nights, both Sunday sessions and Monday day). The Billie Jean King U.S. Tennis Center is basically across the street from the Mets' home – then Shea Stadium, now Citi Field.

What were the impressions (my second trip to NYC)? It's big, it's crowded, and I wouldn't want to be there all the time. But there is also a certain energy. Those sentiments apply to both the city and the tournament. It was a good hike to reach our seats in the cavernous Arthur Ashe Stadium (23,000-plus capacity), but a Federer or Agassi match, for example, would produce a tremendous environment.

At that time, Louis Armstrong Stadium and the adjacent Grandstand were the best combination to watch matches. Both were far more intimate than Ashe. You could position yourself to view the action on both courts by taking just a few steps.

One of the most memorable matches from that first Grand Slam was a late Sunday afternoon/early evening battle between Thailand's Paradorn Srichaphan and Italy's Davide Sanguinetti. Both were suffering from cramps in extreme heat in the third-round matchup. The crowd seemed to help will both of them to continue on. The Italian took the final two tiebreakers for a five-set victory.

Grand slam No. 2 would come the next year. If I have not included this important fact already, Karen was born in England. Parents Gordon and Shelagh moved, first to Canada and then Chicago later the same year, but family members remained in London, Manchester and Scotland, among other places.

The Schuman family vacation in 2006 was to include stops with cousins in all the locations noted above. I honestly don't remember if the vacation was planned first and we then noticed it would be the same time as Wimbledon, or we purposely planned the timing around the tennis tournament. Most who know me would say the latter, but Karen, as nearly always, was in charge of the logistics.

Wimbledon is the only major that on the second Monday plays all of the round of 16 matches. That makes for a very busy day and one in which it would be difficult to get a ticket. We opted to try and go the next day – July 4, 2006 – which would feature the women's quarterfinals. Megan (age 14) and Josh (7) did not share the same enthusiasm as Karen and I, but they were coming along.

We left Karen's cousin's house in the wee hours of the morning to take a subway, then a bus to the Wimbledon village. We would then enter the queue – as the Brits say – to determine if we would be able to get tickets. After a lengthy wait, we approached the front of the line and were asked if we wanted to purchase center court tickets. Since this would likely fall in the once-in-a-lifetime scenario, we quickly said yes and shelled out more than $500 (cash only).

It was a record hot day in London. We watched some outer court play before proceeding to the feature matches that included victories from Maria Sharapova and Kim Clijsters. Both kids were caught dosing during a doubles match featuring American stars Bob and Mike Bryan. And, as an added bonus, we were witnesses to a streaker entering the court at one point before being whisked away by security.

All in all, an outstanding day.

We returned to the U.S. Open in 2015 and 2019 for similar Labor Day weekend matches. Gordon and Shelagh came along the second time, after discovering a year earlier that this tennis thing wasn't too bad. The Arthur Ashe Stadium roof that was under construction in 2015 and fully in place four years later certainly is good for continued play in rainy weather but doesn't help, in my view, the atmosphere. Bottom line: The facility is just too big.

The Happy Slam

It's not easy to get away to go to Australia in the middle of January. But the right time finally came in 2018. Karen's parents opted to make the long trip also to see a country they had not had the opportunity to visit.

The Australian Open is called the Happy Slam. And that's exactly what we experienced. People from throughout Asia and beyond are just excited to be in the land down under. As the locals says to anything that arises, "No worries, mate."

In addition to three days of tennis, we had a tremendous bonus thrown in. The English and Australian national cricket teams were going to be playing a series of matches at the same time. My in-laws never thought they would once again see one of the sports they had grown up watching in England.

We met in Los Angeles for a 15-hour flight to Sydney, then a connection to Melbourne. We dropped our bags at the hotel and walked to the nearby Melbourne Cricket Ground, built in 1853 and with an attendance record of more than 93,000 for a 2015 World Cup final. As you know by now, Karen and I will give just about any sport a try. We knew nothing about cricket, though, so it took some coaching for us to understand the game. But there was no mistaking the passion in the stands through chants, songs, cheers and more.

We arrived late and left early, which is rare for the Schumans. But it was not from a lack of interest. The match and the atmosphere were fascinating. And Shelagh, who sometimes was known for taking puzzle books with her to other sporting events, seemed to enjoy this as much as Gordon.

It was on to tennis (Melbourne Park was located next to the cricket ground) for three days. The smaller venues (Rod Laver and Margaret Court stadiums) allow for excellent viewing. The third show court, Hisense Arena that year, was the preferred court of local favorite Nick Kyrgios. A night match there with the temperamental Kyrgios delivered a raucous atmosphere.

Following that match, we shifted to a smaller venue for a late night special between rising Russian Andre Rublev and veteran Marcos Baghdatis. The fans from the small island of Cyprus tried to will the soon-to-be-retiring Baghdatis to victory but were unsuccessful. Similar to the Srichiphan-Sanguinetti matchup 13 years earlier in New York, this was a classic due to the crowd and the passion.

Sitting at the airport the next day for a short trip to Canberra, we noticed the cricket battle would be shifting to Sydney later in the week (at a time when we would be there). We bought tickets and took in our second cricket contest a few days later. The Sydney Cricket Ground is another historical venue, making for an additional experience to remember.

An effort to complete our Grand Slam with a trip to Paris and the French Open in 2023 was put on hold by my broken foot. But we're confident that day will soon come.

Enjoying one of our two trips – so far – to the Australian Open.

Once-in-a-lifetime visits to the historic cricket grounds in Melbourne and Sydney.

CHAPTER 17

The 2022 Trifecta

The introduction of this book cited the 2022 trifecta. Without any further delay, that would be the 2022 World Men's Curling Championship in Las Vegas; the NCAA Men's College World Series in Omaha and the World Athletics Championships in Eugene, Oregon.

Curling is officially described as a "sport in which players slide stones on a sheet of ice toward a target area which is segmented into four concentric circles." It is typically relegated to that once-ever-four-years Winter Olympics viewing experience. But not for the Schumans.

In fact, after one of those Olympic surges in interest, Karen surprised me with a single-class lesson and curling outing at a local rink near Indianapolis. The simple takeaways from that outing: the approximately 40-pound stones are quite difficult to throw but it really didn't matter that much as we were more concerned with not falling flat on our face on the ice.

We watched our share of curling from the 2022 Olympic Games in Beijing in early February. It was noted during the broadcast that the men's world championships would follow in a few months. A quick search found the site would be Las Vegas in early April, which just happened to be the same time we would be there celebrating my in-laws' 60th wedding anniversary.

On April 8, our destination was the Orleans Arena for one of the final rounds of preliminary play. We were joined by a few thousand fans, mostly Canadians who were seemingly making Las Vegas their second home. Scottish fans were fewer in number but pulled off one of the better feats. In a world in which event security typically precludes bringing in anything larger than a small, clear plastic bag, several pulled out large booming bagpipes to serenade their squad.

The Canadians defeated the Scots, and the U.S. topped Finland in the two matches we focused on most. The strategic discussions and the precision of the players was even more evident in person. Add in the raucous fans and this was another event that more than lived up to expectations.

Omaha and the College World Series (CWS) was a bucket list item of mine for many years. Sure, there was the baseball but once again a major part of the attraction was the way the city had embraced this event for more than 70 years. One day after the Field of Dreams stop, we were in the outfield bleachers at Charles Schwab Field for a bracket final between undefeated Mississippi and Southeastern Conference rival Arkansas.

One of the first sights in walking around downtown Omaha was the many Razorback fans sporting their "Omahogs" shirts. They were not to be outdone by the Rebels and their "OleMaha" attire.

In Iowa the day before, we had encountered two Ole Miss fans who had made the 300-mile trip to the Field of Dreams from Omaha on an off day for their team. They explained Ole Miss's losing record halfway through the conference season and the pitching revival (led by a freshman and a transfer) that had brought them from one of the last four teams in the tournament to the final three at that point.

A second set of fans in Iowa was there after attending the first seven games in Omaha. They were supporting the University of Texas, which was eliminated with two early losses. The man, who worked at the university and was a former high school baseball coach, admitted that one of his goals was to view the entire CWS in person.

I, on the other hand, was content with just the one game. We saw a 3-2 Arkansas win, forcing a second game to determine the bracket winner. Mississippi earned revenge the next day, 2-0, and went on to upset favored Oklahoma in two straight in the best-of-three championship series.

The CWS is an annual tradition in Omaha and the curling championships had actually made one prior stop in Las Vegas. The third leg of our trifecta, however, was remarkably coming to the United States for the first time. I had spotted this the year prior. With our retirement to Arizona, a first-ever trip to Oregon was certainly in the realm of possibility. The gathering of the world's best in track and field, officially known as the World Athletics Championships, had debuted in 1983 in Finland; the 2022 version would be the 15th installment.

Eugene, Oregon has earned the title of TrackTown USA. The city, the University of Oregon and its Hayward Field facility have hosted NCAA and national championships, U.S. Olympic Trials and more. The new Hayward Field, rebuilt on the site of the former stadium and completed in 2020, is a theater-type setting with the fans (with nearly 25,000 seats available for this event) close to the track and with outstanding views of the action.

The university and community are passionate about the sport. While Indianapolis rightfully claims to be the country's amateur sports capital, it must yield to Eugene when it comes to this sport.

We secured tickets for the night session on day eight of the 10-day event. There was a good mix of finals, heats and field events taking place.

Similar to the curling event earlier in the year, we saw a mix of international flags and enthusiastic supporters from around the world. Two young Canadians in our section were determined to attract the attention of sprinter Andre De Grasse.

We witnessed heat races in the men's and women's 4X100 relays. The fast pace of those events, often coming down to execution of the crucial baton exchanges, is always a favorite. Canada, with De Grasse on the anchor leg, upset the U.S. in the men's final when one of those exchanges for the Americans was not as seamless as it needed to be.

Pole vault preliminaries kicked off our night and continued throughout the program. While two Americans exited early, eventual silver medal winner Chris Nilsen advanced. We also saw the current leader in the sport, Sweden's Mondo Duplantis, who went on to set a world record in the finals.

The women's javelin final was a little more difficult to follow. But we were treated to another of the meet's highlights as American Kara Winger, in her final major event, unleashed a throw of more than 64 meters on her final attempt to move from fifth place to second. She took her time circling the track, draped in an American flag, in an emotional celebration.

In an extremely close men's 400 meters, Michael Norman of the U.S. held off five challengers that all finished within one second. Norman had suffered through a series of disappointing finishes in major events in recent years.

The session closed with a highly anticipated women's 400-meter hurdles rematch. At the Tokyo Olympics in 2021, Sydney McLaughlin of the U.S. barely edged teammate Dalilah Muhammad. The two had dominated the event in recent years, setting a series of records in the process.

This time around, McLaughlin left do doubt. While it's sometimes difficult to judge who is actually in front in such events when there is a staggered start and runners must stay in their lanes, McLaughlin had clearly made up the stagger by the halfway mark. She cruised to victory in 50.68 seconds, lowering her own world record by nearly three-quarters of a second, Muhammad finished third.

In one of the more incredible stats I've ever seen, McLaughlin's time was only one and a half seconds slower than the winning time in the women's 400-meter finals. She ran the same distance, with the not insignificant addition of 10 hurdles along the way. It was one of those rare dominating performances that leaves you in a bit of awe.

It was another successful chapter in our sports journey. While on the road the following day, Karen and I shared that while we enjoyed the trifecta (well, maybe me a little more than her), the top event for both of us was the curling.

Back to the Diamonds

The tour of all the major league baseball stadiums outlined in Chapter 12 also came to a close in 2022. Kansas City was part of the Field of Dreams and College World Series trip. Seattle and Oakland followed the track and field championships in Oregon. Finally, Atlanta, Tampa and Miami were sandwiched around a September cruise embarking from Florida.

Kansas City certainly fell into the pleasant surprise category. Kauffman Stadium was celebrating its 50th anniversary, but major renovations in 2009 had paid huge dividends. The Royals Hall of Fame was part of that upgrade. It did a spectacular job telling the story of the franchise's beginnings, the community spirit that elevated it, the World Series titles of 1985 and 2015, and the star players such as George Brett, Frank White, Bret Saberhagen and more.

We were among a crowd of 25,000-plus on a Friday night (postgame fireworks were part of the attraction) that witnessed a two-hour, 22-minute pitchers duel won by the home team 3-1. It was a well-played game on a pleasant summer night.

As a bonus, I could go back home to some new friends from the Kansas City area and say we parked our car at adjacent Arrowhead Stadium, and I could practically see where the Bengals' winning field goal sailed through the uprights months earlier to send the team to the Super Bowl.

Bonus number two was a trip earlier that day to the Negro Leagues Baseball Museum. A variety of leagues and barnstorming teams were the only options for talented Black baseball players before Jackie Robinson broke the color barrier in 1947.

Like other museums I have enjoyed, this one told the bigger story. In this case, that involved the state of our country during these times and how society impacted the sport. Of course, there were also some little-known details on the outstanding careers of Satchel Paige, Josh Gibson, Buck O'Neil and many more.

A special purchase was a hat from the Indianapolis Clowns, the team that initially signed Hank Aaron before his Hall of Fame career with the Braves in Milwaukee and Atlanta. If you are in the Kansas City area, a trip to the Negro Leagues Baseball Museum is highly recommended.

Next up was a Seattle-Oakland doubleheader two days apart. About the only thing in common was the Houston Astros serving as the opponent for both.

T-Mobile Park in Seattle was filled with excitement on the Sunday afternoon following the All-Star break. The Mariners had won 14 in a row before the break, then lost two in a row to Houston. But nearly 35,000 fans turned out on a sunny day in the Pacific Northwest.

The Mariners don't have world titles, or even a World Series appearance, in their 45-year history. But the franchise has been home to individual standouts Ken Griffey Jr., Edgar Martinez, Randy Johnson and others. Those careers, as well as the early history of baseball in the city, are spotlighted in a good (not quite to the level of Kansas City) display.

Another positive was an impressive food menu. On this day, that was an acai bowl for Karen and some fish and chips for me. There were other expansive options (garlic fries, clam chowder, etc.) that will have to wait for a future visit.

On the field, we rightfully booed the longtime Astros who were part of the sign stealing scandal when the team won the World Series in 2017. Jose Altuve promptly responded with a first-pitch home run. Jeremy Pena followed with a longball of his own as Houston went on to an 8-5 win.

Two days later, we were in Oakland. I had read a recent story in which baseball commissioner Rob Manfred had declared that the need for a new stadium for the A's was at a desperate point. Well, we quickly found out the commissioner was correct on that one.

Let me count a few of the ways:

- The gates did not even open until one hour before the game. The typical time is 90 minutes (or longer) ahead of the first pitch so fans can enjoy the end of

batting practice, purchase souvenirs, sample concessions or simply enjoy the atmosphere. That was certainly not the case here.

- Karen and I each had our own comparisons for the concrete concourses. I simply termed it dungeon like, while Karen thought it was more like the depths of the New York subway system. No matter which you prefer, I think you get the picture.
- Many of the concession stands were not open. With the ultimate attendance of 5,130, I guess there was no reason to expand the misery.
- There was a salute to franchise history in Oakland – three straight titles in the 1970s (Vida Blue, Rollie Fingers, Reggie Jackson among the stars) and the earthquake-delayed win in 1989 over Bay rival San Francisco. But even those were primarily images and newspaper headlines that covered some of the concrete walls.

The stadium workers were friendly. We talked to one who had worked in sales and sponsorships for more than 20 years. He hoped the proposed downtown location for a new stadium eventually would be approved instead of what later became the plan – following the football Raiders to Las Vegas.

In this game, a third-inning grand slam by Chad Pinder held up for a 5-3 victory for the home team. Oakland won the next day for a three-game sweep. Amazingly, in late July, it was the first series sweep of the season for the A's and the first time the Astros had been swept. You just never know what might happen over a 162-game season.

Early September featured our final three baseball stops. The combination of Friday night fireworks, a Ronald Acuna bobblehead night and a defending world champion Braves team gaining ground on the Mets in the NL East produced a sellout crowd. Five Atlanta home runs in the game, including three off Miami ace Sandy Alcantra, delivered an 8-1 victory.

Truist Park was impressive both outside and in. The move from downtown to suburban Cobb County in 2017 was controversial. But the franchise has constructed a comprehensive entertainment venue – similar to the complex outside Busch Stadium in St. Louis.

Inside, the Braves do an outstanding job of capturing the history of the franchise and its star players. The centerpiece is longtime home run king Aaron and his contributions on the field but, more importantly, in the community. Maybe it's a recency factor – both in the timing of our visit and recent stadium construction – but Truist earns a top five ranking in my book.

One day later, we were in Tampa. Or you could call it Part 1 of the New York invasion. The crowd of 21,000 plus, one of the largest of the season for the Rays, featured more Aaron Judge t-shirts and jerseys than anywhere outside Yankee Stadium. The post-All Star Game swoon for the Bronx Bombers continued with a 2-1 loss. The only run came on Judge's 52nd homer (on the way to 62 for the season) in the top of the ninth.

I chronicled our previous visits to Tropicana Field for the 1999 Final Four and 2012 college football bowl game involving Ball State. The stadium was disappointing then – and nothing changed in the ensuing years. It was like a return to the concrete jungle of Oakland, only with a little color thrown in. The food, activities and atmosphere were all below par at best.

One week later, our long baseball stadium trek came to an end at LoanDeport Park in Miami. This time it was the National League team from New York providing the opposition and cheers of "Let's Go Mets!" dominated the crowd noise throughout the contest. The Marlins, the 8-1 losers in Atlanta eight days earlier, gave up eight runs in the fourth inning of this one in an 11-3 setback.

The Miami franchise moved to LoanDepot, built on the site of the former Orange Bowl, in 2012. The near downtown location is a plus compared to Joe Robbie Stadium (known by a number of names over the years). Locals said the retractable roof is rarely open due to the heat. While comfortable, from a temperature standpoint, on the inside, there is little to set the venue apart from others. Overall, it falls in the mediocre category.

But there was a most fitting end to our journey. It was Karen's idea to take a sign to the game, which I am sure was a first for us. We captured a few of the highlights from our 2022 travels, including a line about the conclusion of our 30-ballpark tour.

In the middle of the fifth inning, I managed to catch the attention of a WPIX (broadcasting the game back to New York) cameraman near the Mets dugout. He focused on our sign, which I held high. He gave me a thumbs up after a lengthy shot – and I responded with the same.

I found the replay of the broadcast a day later through the

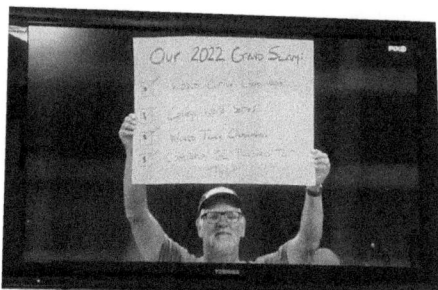

MLB app. I was on camera for maybe five seconds with announcers Gary Cohen, Ron Darling and Keith Hernandez noting the accomplishment of 30 baseball games in 30 cities (believing they all occurred in 2022, but that doesn't take away from the acknowledgement). With the score of the game 10-1 at that point, they also cited the world curling line on the sign and engaged in a several-minute conversation about the sport and its attributes and shortcomings.

Although I did nothing but hold a sign for a few moments, it was a nice way to wrap up a baseball dream.

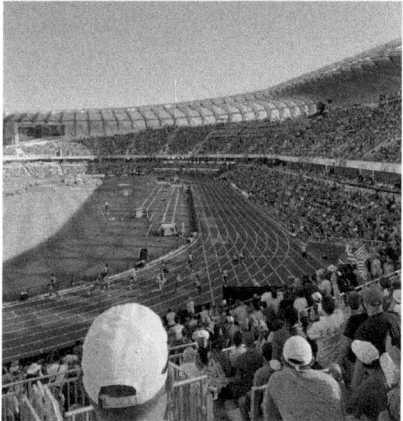

A "world" trifecta in 2022: Curling in Las Vegas, the College World Series in Omaha and the Track Championships in Eugene, Oregon.

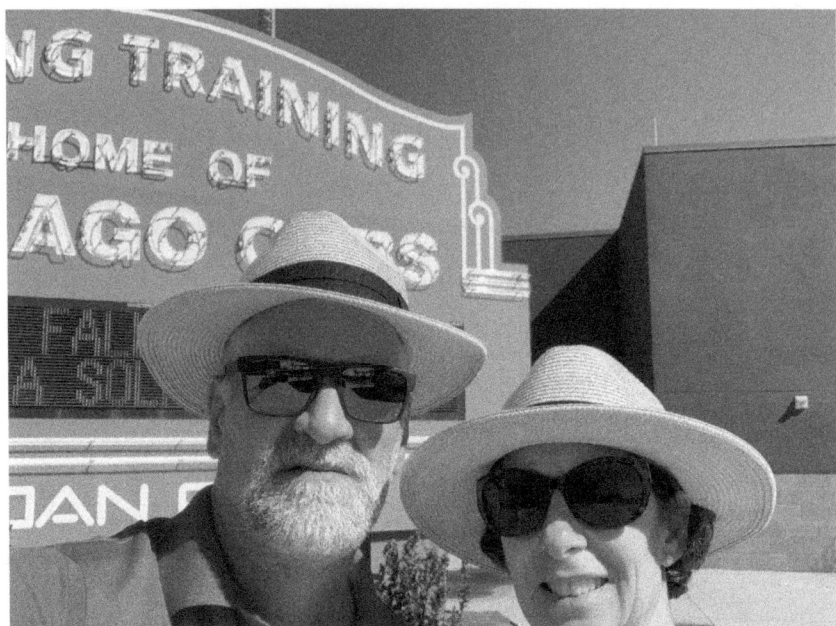

Spring training baseball at the Chicago Cubs home away from home in Mesa, Arizona.

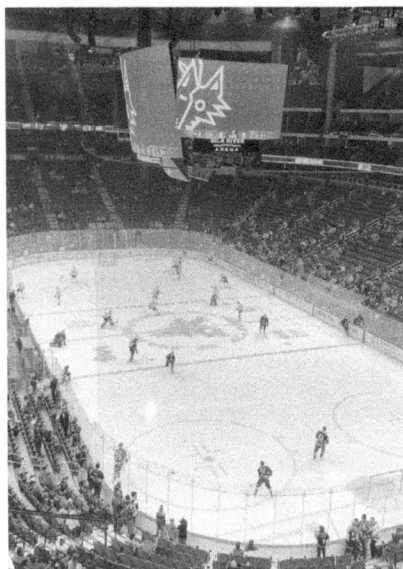

Another Chicago connection – this time with the Blackhawks (and their fans) invading Arizona to take on the Coyotes.

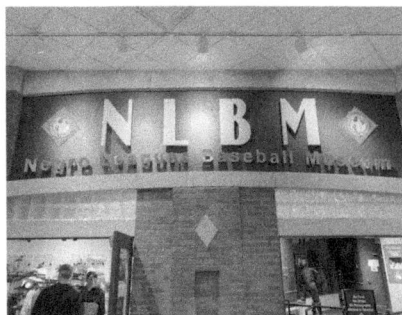

A day at the Negro Leagues Baseball Museum in Kansas City was a special experience.

CHAPTER 18

Sports of All Sorts

We've covered some of the major sports and a few other less common events. But the memories are far from complete.

In the professional basketball world, two games stand out. Both were playoff contests involving the Indiana Pacers, an American Basketball Association (ABA) franchise that was founded in 1967 and merged into the NBA nine years later. The franchise won three ABA titles but has only advanced to one NBA finals in 47 years. That was in 2000 against the Los Angeles Lakers of Shaquille O'Neal and Kobe Bryant.

Karen managed to secure two tickets in the lower bowl, about 14 rows up, for the pivotal Game 4 in Indianapolis. The Lakers led 2-1. O'Neal was the primary star at that point, while Bryant had missed most of Game 2 and all of Game 3 with a sprained ankle. The Pacers were led by Reggie Miller, 13 years into his 18-year Hall of Fame career and 7-foot-4 center Rik Smits.

Indiana led by 10 early but had to come from behind to force overtime. With O'Neal fouling out after scoring 36 points, the 21-year-old Bryant took over. He played 47 of the 53 minutes and his three key baskets (two long jumpers and a putback under the basket) in the extra session gave the Lakers a 120-118 win and a 3-1 lead in the series. The Pacers bounced back with a 33-point thrashing in Game 5, but the Lakers closed out the series back in L.A. for the first of their three straight championships.

Despite the loss for the home team, it was an outstanding game and seemingly a turning point for the Lakers with Bryant excelling in the clutch.

Five years earlier, on Memorial Day in 1995, another Game 4 went the way of the Pacers. It was the Eastern Conference finals in a steamy and loud Market Square Arena against Orlando. O'Neal was generally a dominating presence for the Magic. But not in this game as he fouled out with only 16 points and 10 rebounds.

Miller gave the home team a two-point lead by nailing a three-pointer with 13.3 left. Penny Hardaway responded with an off-balance three of his own to put Orlando back into the lead. But after a series of timeouts, the Pacers inbounded to Smits, who faked before knocking down a 15-foot jumper at the buzzer for a 94-93 win. The Magic won that series in seven games.

A side note that doesn't involve a direct sports experience for me, but one I have always admired. The indirect connection: The Spirits of St. Louis (Bob Costas, our Annual Dinner guest more than two decades later, was once a play-by-play announcer for the colorful Spirits).

When it came time for a merger, the NBA wanted four franchises – Indiana included. The Virginia Squires folded, and the Kentucky Colonels agreed to exit for a $3 million payout. The two brothers who owned the Spirits were in no mood to go away that easily.

The first part of the deal they worked out included $2.2 million for the Spirits of St. Louis players taken by NBA teams in a dispersal draft. In addition, they insisted on a share of the money from the NBA's national TV rights, taking one-seventh of each of the four ex-ABA teams' shares. The key phrase for the second part of the deal – in perpetuity.

This was a relatively insignificant money stream in 1976. Once Magic Johnson and Larry Bird entered the league three years later, followed in short order by Michael Jordan and a host of other stars, NBA television rights became a hot commodity.

From 1977 to 2014, the NBA took in about $15 billion in national TV money from increasingly lucrative contracts with the networks. Per their agreement with the NBA, that earned $300 million for the former Spirits' owners.

Finally, the NBA made an offer too good to refuse: half a billion dollars upfront to surrender all future claims to TV money. The brothers and their lawyer accepted, bringing their total haul to $800 million for doing nothing for 38 years.

In the Crease

I've not lived in a city with a National Hockey League franchise. But that doesn't mean we lack some memorable games on the ice in our viewing repertoire.

The most unique was a January 1, 2019, trip to Notre Dame Stadium for the NHL Winter Classic, a regular season tradition that the NHL established in 2008. Most of the early January contests were in baseball stadiums (Wrigley Field, Fenway Park, etc.). Notre Dame was the second college football host, following Michigan Stadium in 2014.

We were joined by 80,000 others on a cold (it was January 1 in South Bend so anything else would have been an upset) day that also featured a few snow flurries. Boston defeated Chicago 4-2 but the score or the outcome really didn't matter. We were there for another special event.

We had been to previous Blackhawks games (part of Karen's Chicago roots) in Chicago and even in Columbus, Ohio. I love watching hockey, especially in the playoffs, on TV but you can see so much more in person with the view of the entire ice. And in those playoffs, the handshake line at the end of the series is always a great sight. The same men that have battled each other in every way possible engage in a sincere display of mutual respect.

There have been more than a few minor league franchises in Indianapolis. No matter the league or the affiliation, intense rivalries exist with geographic foes Fort Wayne and/or Cincinnati. And as in other sports, those running minor league clubs must be creative to be sure to continue to put fans in the seats.

That backfired in one game in Fort Wayne between the local Komets and Indianapolis. I'm sure Ice Scraper Night seemed like a good idea when it was discussed. But mix a few controversial calls with some tussles on the ice and those scrapers quickly become flying projectiles. The teams escaped to the locker rooms, the cleanup crews went to work and the few minutes remaining in the second period were added to the third stanza.

At the Track

I noted earlier that Karen and I attended the first 17 NASCAR races at Indianapolis Motor Speedway. While that venue is known worldwide, the better racing actually took part at nearby Indianapolis Raceway Park (IRP). The short track oval (.686 miles) featured both trucks and the then Busch series cars in lead-ins to the Brickyard 400.

It became a ritual to enter IRP as soon as it opened on Saturday afternoon to stake out territory on the turn one hill. A small tarp and a couple of chairs would ensure us a prime location for that night's main event. We would return about six hours later for qualifying and the race. Forty-three cars on that short track never failed in delivering on excitement.

The NASCAR fandom led to three road trips in the 1998-2000 period. The destinations were Martinsville, Virginia (shortest track on the circuit), Talladega, Alabama (the largest superspeedway) and Charlotte, North Carolina (the longest race in the Coca Cola 600 on Memorial Day weekend).

A quick memory from each:

- John Andretti, who made Indianapolis his adopted home as part of a career that also included IndyCar, won at Martinsville for Richard Petty Racing in a pit stop strategy battle. Andretti was a truly good guy in the sport who passed away way too young due to prostate cancer.
- I assume most of us, at one time or another, have forgotten where we parked our car. It's a bad idea to do so when you have a rental outside a facility that sits on nearly 3,000 acres of land. Add in the expected traffic once we located the vehicle, and it turned into a hectic return to the Birmingham airport. Thankfully, in those days, it was easier to return the rental, clear security and dash to the gate to catch the flight.
- In Charlotte, we experienced rain delays in what was already a 600-mile marathon. Taking refuge under the stands, attention quickly turned to the fan with the wooden leg. Not any wooden leg, but one with a number and color scheme matching the ride of fan favorite Dale Earnhardt. Only in the home of NASCAR.

On the Pitch

Megan and Josh both played soccer on travel teams, so I had plenty of experience in trying to pick up the intricacies of a sport that was not available when I was a youngster. I even coached them briefly at younger ages, but that was when the primary goal was to try and get everyone moving in the proper direction.

I can't say that I developed the passion for the game that some younger co-workers and friends possessed. But World Cup matches and U.S. national team outings were certainly prime viewing opportunities.

Two quick stories, one via TV and the other in person.

The 2006 trip to England that produced the Wimbledon experience also featured our own United Nations moment. Just prior to the trip to London, we traveled to Scotland to visit with another cousin of Karen's. And we just happened to be there for the World Cup quarterfinal match between England and Portugal.

Josh, born in Russia and now American, was in Scotland supporting cousins he had just met for the first time as England played Portugal in Germany. With stars David Beckham (injured) and Wayne Rooney (red card), not playing, England battled to a 0-0 tie before losing on penalty kicks. Seven-year-old Josh shed a few tears over that one.

By the way, is there any more unsatisfying – or maybe unfair – way to end a major sporting event than with penalty kicks. Hockey does it in the regular season but not in the playoffs. Soccer should follow suit. The penalty kick scenario – used to decide Olympics, World Cups and all other major matches – is like baseball deciding to have a home run battle or basketball being decided on a free throw contest.

The memorable in-person soccer experience came in 2013 when Megan was working on a college internship in Barcelona. Karen, Josh and I managed to visit her along with side trips to Paris and Rome in about 10 days.

Camp Nou is the legendary home of FC Barcelona and then star Lionel Messi, commonly regarded as one of the greatest players of all time. With a seating capacity of more than 99,000, the stadium is the largest facility of its kind in Spain/Europe and fourth largest in the world. We were able to obtain tickets for a Sunday night league match. Nearly 80,000 made their way to the game.

Messi scored a pair of goals in a match dominated by FC Barcelona. Two off-field items that stood out: Visiting team fans were confined to a small section basically protected by chicken wire, while many home team supporters brought with them what can best be described as a picnic basket of snacks (no missing the action while standing in concession lines).

Finally, in both Barcelona and on a later trip to Helsinki, Finland, we visited the primary stadiums used for the 1992 and 1952 Olympics, respectively. It's always interesting to see a little history in person.

Honoring the Greats

History, of course, is the centerpiece of any hall of fame. I have been to two national ones – the professional football version in Canton, Ohio (coming after a baseball trip to Pittsburgh) and the hockey shrine in Toronto (on a visit to see more of Karen's family).

I enjoyed the comprehensiveness in Canton, including a large visual display with won-loss records for every team in every season of the now 100-year-old league. The busts of the Hall of Famers were also an impressive sight.

Hockey seemed to be much more interactive with lots of activities for younger fans. Josh and I were solo on that visit and had a great time.

On a separate trip up north, I was able to attend a Canadian Football League game at the home of the Hamilton Tiger-Cats. It wasn't a particularly memorable contest (the home team was shut out), but I consider it another ingredient on my wide-ranging sports menu.

Two other halls of note. The Green Bay Packers have done it right. Even Karen, a devoted Bears fan who likes nothing about Green Bay, agrees. The history of Lambeau Field itself, as well as the only NFL franchise that is publicly owned, is captured in extensive detail.

Similar to the way the Indianapolis Motor Speedway was only used for the month of May and the Indianapolis 500 for years, Lambeau was a Packers-only destination. That changed in both places, which was a major victory for fans and the communities.

Then there is the Indiana Basketball Hall of Fame, mentioned earlier in my *BizVoice* magazine article. I've said it before – Indiana loves basketball. The rich history, particularly at the high school level, is expertly captured for fans of all ages. Oscar Robertson, George McGinnis, Larry Bird and Damon Bailey are four of the thousands of legendary players. The hall highlights the players, teams and communities that made the sport so special for so many years.

On February 12, 2001, I even attended the annual ESPY awards in Las Vegas. I mention the date because I'm sure I took grief for being in Sin City with a friend (who was attending a veterinarian convention by day) instead of at home on Karen's birthday. Greco-Roman wrestler Rulon Gardner, who won an Olympic gold medal the year before by defeating a Russian who had not lost in 13 years, was one of the stars of that show.

Ring It Up

Is professional wrestling a sport? I will admit that's debatable. But there's no questioning the athletic ability of the participants. Many found their way to the ring after careers on the football field or in other sports. And I've been a longtime wrestling fan. I don't watch any reality TV shows, so maybe some occasional wrestling viewing takes its place.

I've attended several World Wresting Entertainment (WWE) events in person. The first, with a Wabash co-worker and our spouses, was a regular touring event in Fort Wayne. Rowdy Roddy Piper was one of the headliners on that card.

The second WWE foray was a big one. As in Wrestlemania VIII (if you use Roman numerals like the Super Bowl, it has to be big, correct?) at the RCA Dome in Indianapolis in April 1992. The co-headliner matches: Hulk Hogan vs. Sid Justice and Ric Flair vs. Macho Man Randy Savage. Best friend Kirk and our wives (they must really love us) were among 62,000 in attendance.

WWE puts on great shows. It's no so much about who wins that week as there is always another match to come. It's all about the storytelling and the athleticism. The performers and the writers do both of those very well.

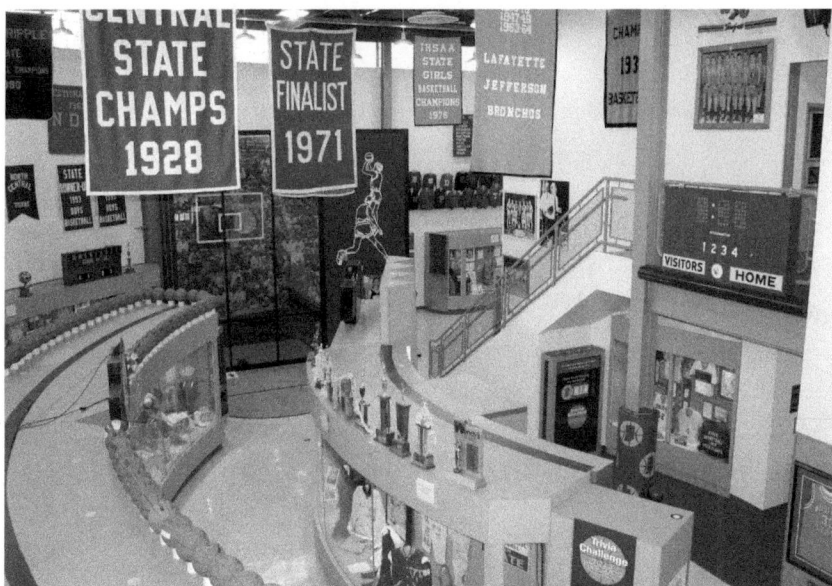

One can spend many hours in the Indiana Basketball Hall of Fame.

With the family at a 2013 soccer game at the famed Camp Nou in Barcelona.

The Winter Classic hockey game between Chicago and Boston at Notre Dame's football stadium.

It was a cold, windy day in December 2019 – big surprise – at Green Bay's Lambeau Field.

EPILOGUE

This book primarily, and with good reason, focuses on events I reported on, attended or otherwise experienced as a fan. The personal playing experience is somewhat limited and far less exciting. I opened with a few examples, however, and will close with these athletic pursuits.

Softball: With my early baseball days over rather quickly, I turned to softball as a teen and played recreationally for most of the next 30 years. That includes summertime leagues at home, a few championships with some talented friends at Ball State, a long run with co-workers and others while in Anderson and both co-ed and men's play in Indianapolis.

While working at the newspaper in Anderson, I would take my "dinner hour" to head to the diamond for a game before returning to finish the night's work. Driving to the game, playing and coming back could not be accomplished in 60 minutes, so it was good that my bosses were understanding as long as the job got done on time.

I was a left-handed hitter who, during those days, could run a little bit. Slapping the ball down the left field line and turning it into a double or triple was always a lot of fun. The results were usually mixed but good times with good friends could not be beat.

When I was in my mid-40s, I played first base with two older friends doing the pitching and catching. I think the three "seniors" on the team held our own, but sons (of the other two) and their friends supplied the power and fielding we needed to win a couple of titles.

Running: This is certainly the outlier. Yes, I just said I was able to take a few extra bases on the softball diamond during my younger days. That certainly would not translate to any type of distance running.

But in May 2004, watching the annual 500 Festival Mini-Marathon that opened the month of May in Indianapolis, I saw a woman in her early 80s cross the finish line. My comment to Karen: "If this woman can do that, certainly we (40 years younger) can."

That started a 12-month journey that is not often fondly remembered by my lovely wife. If we were going to pull this off, it was going to take training – and a lot of it. We followed a program as close as possible, extending our distances as we moved closer to the following May. On one rainy Saturday, when we were scheduled for a nearly 10-mile run, we were relegated to an indoor facility with a one-eighth mile track. Shortly after beginning, my off-handed comment that we only had 288 more turns on the short track was not well received.

The Indianapolis event was one of the larger half marathons in the country. The 13.2-mile race begins downtown, winds through several neighborhoods, includes a lap around the legendary Indianapolis Motor Speedway and returns back downtown. One of Karen's favorite observations to this day was that upon exiting the Speedway, we were almost as close to home as we were to the conclusion of the race. She had to convince herself to make the proper turn and stay on course.

I recall a finishing time of two hours and 26 minutes, which was nothing to write home about. But the sense of accomplishment was immense. I also recall needing to leave rather quickly to go coach one of Josh's soccer games. Most of the time there was spent sitting on the ground and fighting off the leg cramps that persisted for several days.

Pickleball: I first heard about pickleball in 2017 at the NCAA Final Four in Phoenix. Dave Carrington is the father of fellow Ball State grad Brett, my Indiana Chamber colleague and good friend for more than 20 years. Dave was our host that weekend at his winter residence in Mesa. He was bemoaning the fact that he was being assessed a fee for the construction of new pickleball courts in his community.

The next exposure to the fast-growing sports was when Karen and I moved to Maricopa in June 2021 and retired two months later. We ventured to the pickleball courts and quickly met some of the nicest people in the world. I soon became addicted (Karen less so, though she is an outstanding player), competing in a league in early 2022, adding tournaments to the slate late (winning a few early titles) in the year and playing an average of three hours a day every day.

Where this experience will lead is yet to be seen. I do know pickleball has helped me become healthier than I have been in years. I'm confident the fun and competitive nature will play a role in keeping me young at heart.

For now, we will simply term it the next chapter in *My Wide World of Sports*.

Pickleball play has become an almost daily obsession –
with a few tournament rewards for the efforts.

A memento for finishing the 13.1
Indianapolis 500 Festival Mini-Marathon.

A Constant Variety of Sports

The world of sports touches our lives in so many ways. Most of us played some version of the games in our younger days. Even more become ardent supporters of their favorite teams. Some take to the road to view the contests in person, while others practice their fandom from afar.

I qualify for all of the above. In addition, I have spent a total of 45 years as a journalist – sportswriter, newspaper staffer and magazine editor. In each of these roles, and beyond, I accumulated fascinating stories about the games, personalities and experiences.

Yes, we've got hoops' tales from basketball-crazy Indiana and the ups – and mostly downs – from professional teams in Cincinnati. We mix in global tennis and soccer adventures and everything from hockey and golf to cricket and curling.

The individuals encountered, to name a few, include Bob Knight, Lou Holtz, Jack Nicklaus, Tom Brokaw, Carl Erskine, Pete and Alice Dye and many more. The big games include multiple NCAA Final Fours, the World Series and Super Bowl.

I have spent most of my life telling others' stories. Along the way, I've accumulated a few anecdotes of my own that I'm confident you will enjoy.

About the Author

Tom Schuman worked 13 years as a newspaper reporter and editor, and 23 years in communications with the Indiana Chamber of Commerce. Tom and Karen live in Maricopa, Arizona, and still travel far and wide to various sporting events.

Back Cover
Celebrating the conclusion of a whirlwind 2022 in Miami.

Milton Keynes UK
Ingram Content Group UK Ltd.
UKHW050517010324
438641UK00003B/5

9 798218 353919